ABU TALKS

NORMAN HUNT
*Founder and leader of the
Norman Hunt Circles.*

W. F. RICKARD
The Instrument.

ABU TALKS

VOLUME ONE

—

THE ABU TRUST

Regency Press (London & New York) Ltd.
125 High Holborn, London WC1V 6QA

ISBN 0 7212 0882 7

Printed and bound in Great Britain by
Buckland Press Ltd., Dover, Kent.

CONTENTS

FOREWORD

For years my father, Norman Hunt, studied philosophy, religion and art, reaching a plane of understanding which most of us cannot hope to attain. My wife and I were privileged to be present on many occasions as members of his psychic circles, which operated for fourteen years from 1949 in Tunbridge Wells and Pembury, Kent. The majority of the sittings were tape recorded, and constitute an incredible portfolio of beautiful religious principles, and discussion of topical questions. This book carries a portion of this teaching, which was obtained by Frances Atlee, a skilled stenographer now deceased, who was also a circle member.

I must first explain that the way in which this advanced yet simple teaching came to us was through a "medium" in deep trance, which is a state of complete voluntary unconsciousness. Its occurrence is very rare and of immense value, since it permits conversation to take place between ourselves on earth, and those in spirit who wish to talk to us.

The "medium" was W.F. (Rick) Rickard, a man of warm heart and great intellect, who my parents met in 1948, and who with his wife had also been interested and involved in communication through a psychic circle in Kent. The rapport between them was immediate. Not long after that time, "Rick" began to go into trance frequently, and the need to record the teaching became paramount. Whilst in trance "Rick" was totally unaware of anything which took place, and awoke as from a normal sleep, yet without any recollection of what had taken place.

Through "Rick", many people from different backgrounds and races came to our weekly circles, but the major personality and teacher was affectionately known to us as ABU, whose earthly life took place over 3,000 years ago in Egypt, where he was a member of the priesthood. Now residing on a spiritual plane far above our earth, he describes in great detail his experiences after leaving this life. The beauty and sincerity of his message is absolute, which is that LOVE is the source of our being, and the principle by which we should live our lives. In his teachings – and answers to questions – ABU always conveys a great warmth of love, compassion, tolerance and understanding of our difficulties and struggles on earth.

The contents of this book are an accurate and completely un-edited record of some of the teaching brought to the circles in the early stages of their existence. Later sessions were all tape recorded and most of these have been rescued from oblivion by the dedicated and altruistic work of James and Shirley Webster in Battle. They have now converted the original reel tapes to modern cassettes, copies of which are available from them.

I would like to pay particular tribute to this husband and wife team for all their hard work with the tapes, their initiative in the publication of this book, for their concern to help others with this material, and for the privilege of their warm friendship.

John Hunt,
October, 1991.

INTRODUCTION

It was fifteen years ago when we were introduced to the Abu teachings. Ron and Peggy Mason, who were then living in Crowborough, Sussex, had arranged listening and discussion evenings which we regularly attended.

Right from the first listening of these amazing recordings, we knew they were special and the finest and most profound of anything we had come across during the previous twenty or so years spent in paranormal research. We felt this fine teaching of spiritual philosophy deserved to reach a wider audience.

Fortunately, Peggy Mason had carefully copied one hundred and twelve hours of material from the original tape spools recorded at some of the circle 'sittings' during the fourteen years of dedicated service by the members. These, plus five volumes of transcriptions, were very kindly handed over to us.

We have spent several years listening, studying and researching into the activities and results of the Norman Hunt Circles and would like to acknowledge our grateful thanks to Ron and Peggy Mason, the Hunt family, Rosalie Rickard (the mediums' wife) and Peter Jubb for their help, encouragement and co-operation, in providing so much useful information in our research, without which this book and the tapes could not have been produced.

A series of cassette tapes are now available from The Abu Trust. (See advertisement at the back of this book).

THE ABU TRUST
James and Shirley Webster.
(Trustees)

8

Chapter One

ABU'S "CREDENTIALS"

Abu. Communion such as this is a true communion, for it is a communion of hearts and of minds, and the flame which is to us a reality burns the brighter when many shall join together in this manner and unite their common effort.

It assists, as you will understand, upon a somewhat lower level, in the provision of the psychic power which is necessary in order that contact may be made, for that is the case no matter how or when or where a contact shall be made between the world of spirit and the world of flesh. Always, upon every occasion, it is necessary to make use of what you and we alike designate as psychic power, which is a kind of go-between, as it were, partaking somewhat of the nature of both worlds.

Truly it has been said that when two or three are gathered together, there in the midst can be a presence – whether that of the one who spoke those words or that of another I am not in a position to say, but most certainly, where two or three are gathered together there will be a presence. It is the unison, the union and the harmony which make such gatherings as these happy occurrences upon both sides of the division line between us.

I am a mouthpiece; there are many behind me. I use an instrument here who again is a sort of mouthpiece, for it is through his physical mouth that my words emerge. I am of no more importance than is he at this present moment, and of no less. You are not to think that you will be addressed by some person who is to be regarded as "holy" in the sense of being separated and set apart; that is not so. I am man, I was man, and at least for a very long time to be I shall continue to be man, even as you are man and woman.

I am a dead man: that is the only difference, and I have been what the world calls dead for quite a long time; and if one shall live, even upon the earth-plane, for a long period of years, and shall use some endeavour to attain experiences, then those experiences will add to the fullness of the personality. And that is my position and it is my sole authority.

My sole authority in addressing you lies in the fact that I have been dead for a very long time. I have undergone experiences, some happy, some a little less happy and some transcendental, during that period, which I do not measure in years for it would be fruitless so to do, but which I do venture to measure in terms of depth and width of experience. And from that experience I permit myself to speak among you, but I am still only a man. When I present to you ideas and propositions, they are based upon my experiences and I ask that you will pass them under review. If you shall find them acceptable ones, it is well; for, you see, I do not need any conviction *myself* as to my own "worthiness" to speak in this manner for I have undergone these experiences personally: they are part of me, and therefore *I* know that I am right, but I would not wish that you should be required to assent to the proposition that I *am* right without passing what I have to say under review.

9

Chapter Two

MATERIALISM v TEACHINGS OF THE SPIRIT WORLD

Questioner. Commencing about one hundred years ago scientific materialism really began to forge ahead and has somewhat overwhelmed orthodox religions in the western hemispheres. It would appear that efforts made about the same time by the spirit side of life to contact us in a more general way, may have been an effort to combat this wave of materialism. The struggle is still going on. Can you give us any idea of the progress being made, as you see it, and the lines along which it may or will develop?

Abu. You have stated that about a hundred years ago, (in point of fact I think it was rather earlier), the orthodoxy of science found itself in conflict with the orthodoxy of religion, largely because the orthodoxy of science found itself impelled, compelled in fact, along a materialistic channel, for the perfectly sufficient reason that the scientists in their investigations found material things, and could occupy themselves with material things, and they were not required nor compelled by their investigations even to admit the *existence* of anything other than the material things which they were engaged upon investigating. It is a reasonable attitude of mind; it is not an incredulity, it is not a scepticism, provided always that the mind is kept open, it is merely a *scientific* turn of mind. You will understand that when I use the word 'scientific' I am referring primarily to the root of the word, a desire to know and nothing else, and since these materialistic scientists of whom you speak did not find themselves compelled to have regard to any supra-mundane 'attachments' to the material which they were examining and investigating, but did find, on the contrary, a vast number of facts which they could tabulate, associated with that same material, they were acting quite scientifically in not investigating the mystical, (the supra-mundane I have called it), the 'psychic' aspect, of these very things, and they were more justified therein because of the attitude which had been adopted for a long, long period by the orthodox religions.

For the orthodox religions, as you will agree, had (and I think to a large degree still have) taken their stand upon the basis of a unique revelation, which might not be added to nor taken from. It was a complete and a final revelation, nothing might be added thereto, and it must not be questioned. The attitude of a closed mind, a mind completely closed, not only to the possibilities of an enlargement and a widening of the horizon, but convinced of the 'sinfulness' of any such proceedings, must necessarily have run quite counter to the scientific attitude of the more intelligent men who were investigating the matter of which your universe is composed, and so this conflict was in existence immediately the two modes of thought were contemporary. But of course the position had arisen considerably earlier than the "one hundred" or even two hundred years, and since the orthodox religions were so vastly powerful in the earlier days, they were able by force and by fear to suppress the investigations which, a little timorously perhaps, might have been made by aspiring minds which were not content to be walled in to the citadel of orthodoxy but insisted upon knocking a brick out of the edifice in order to see, not *what* there was beyond it, but if there was anything at all beyond it.

But the churches were powerful enough to restrain this process – this so desirable process – for a long, long, time, by the exercise, as I have said, of force and of fear. Eventually the scientific mind became emancipated therefrom, as the sociological mind of man became broader and more humane, in the true and full sense of the word, so that the orthodox religion, the churches, were no longer *allowed* by the broader outlook of governing man, to pronounce sentence of death, of torture, of burning, upon this one and upon that just because this one and that had offended against the tenets of the church, though not against the laws of the state. The two were separable and were separated – did become separated – to a degree, and that opened the possibility for the scientific mind to proceed with its investigation, untrammelled by the forces and the fear which had hitherto been exercised and which had inhibited such investigation.

I do not recognise the spirit of scientific enquiry as in any sense an evil thing. But I do recognise as a foolish, as an unwise thing, *any* form of orthodoxy which results in a closure of the mind. The scientist who refuses to examine is not acting as a scientist, he is acting as a hidebound orthodox person, who is as creed-bound, as you have said, as the persons who have adhered to orthodox religion and would admit nothing else. But that is not science. And I have welcomed the intrusion of 'materialism', for the violent swing of the pendulum, the violent and sudden reversal of the ideas of thinking and intelligent men, was necessary, *was* necessary and at the moment still is necessary; for this reason, that, had the message from the spirit world – (which is the same message as I can never tire of impressing upon you, it is the same message as the churches should have borne to mankind throughout and they have not done so) – but had that message from the spirit world been brought in and persuaded to infiltrate into the existent channels of orthodox religion, the message would again have been smothered and lost, and therefore there was no good purpose, to be served, by handing this 'jewel' to the very people who had already besmirched it and ultimately hidden its light from mankind almost completely.

Therefore I cannot regard the scientific revolution as an evil thing; it was necessary. For, only by such a shocking blow, by an attack with the force of science, an attack upon man's belief – his very belief in God – only by such a shocking blow could man have been divorced from the power of the church and of its grip which tended to keep mankind in darkness for so long and would still have done so.

Then – at this hundred year period of which you speak – we have this split, the necessary split, with the church; the orthodox church, gradually losing its grip upon mankind as the mind of man became emancipated and educated, and with science getting a firmer grip upon that same mind, for exactly the same reasons and apparently in a completely opposed and opposite direction; so that the scientists of that day would have said, without a doubt, that if they had not already proved that there was no God, because there could be no God, and that following thereupon there was no spirit of man, that there was no survival after the death of the physical body, the investigating scientists of those days were of opinion that they had all but reached such a point. And the impact of the spirit world was not made upon the scientists, for it would have been as futile to appeal to them as to appeal to the churches.

11

The appeal from the spirit world was made in a more simple manner to the hearts of more simple people. But eventually of course the facts of the phenomena which were produced from the spirit side of life and the philosophy which was taught and still is taught from the spirit side of life necessarily came under the judgment of, firstly the church, which declared it 'anathema and of the devil', as was to be expected, and then of the scientists, who, were justified in saying "this thing cannot be". But there were and there still are among the scientists men of sufficient intelligence and reasonable faculties as to say, "this thing cannot be and yet it happens, therefore will I investigate". And many of them have found that, in the words of your dramatist, there are more things in heaven and earth than they dreamed of, and many of them of high standing have been sufficiently honest, to proclaim that truth. So that the facts of spirit-return, the survival of man, communication, the progression of the spirit – all these things of which we speak together – now stand upon a basis which is quite unassailable.

For if one shall assail any particular feature of the edifice he shall find that some person, not necessarily a scientist, but some person of reputation, will assert that such and such supports the suggestion, and it is difficult, if not impossible to refute them; and it will be found upon investigation that that applies to the whole of the phenomenal side of what you know as 'spiritualism'. The phenomenal side is established beyond question, without a doubt. Then follow, from the phenomenal side, implications which are philosophical and may be religious, according to the taste of the inquirer. For no one among us would wish to force upon an inquirer a philosophy or a religious view which would be abhorrent to him or to her, we merely wish to lay before you, firstly the facts as opposed to certain theories propounded, (again I regret I have to say by the churches) *facts* which are within our knowledge and are not mere guesses, and secondly to request this investigator, this inquirer, to ponder upon the necessity that there will be, there must be, implications underlying the phenomena. What the inquirer will make of such implications is a matter for the inquirer, and not for us.

You, have done me the honour to place your hands in mine and to accept in a little degree the things which I have told you, the philosophies which I have ventured to lay before you, and you have found them to your taste, and I am happy that it should be so, but you will admit that I have never required of you that you shall accept this or accept that; I may not do so.

We have dealt then with the split, the conflict, we have dealt with the reasons, the necessity, for the swing of the pendulum, we have dealt with the establishment of the impact from the spirit world upon the earth world and the fact that that impact now stands quite reasonably well supported. Now, your scientist has advanced and advanced in his own subject, keeping his eyes rigourously fixed upon the earth and rigourously fixed away from heaven, (whether he in his own mind assented to an idea of heaven or of spirit, or whether he did not, is not material), his investigations were bent upon the things of life. And I will put the questions to you, where has he now arrived? Has he still got his solid material, which is so obviously *not* of the nature of spirit, or has he found something other than that?

Questioner. He has gone quite a long way in another direction though still

12

having certain 'reservations'.

Abu. Would you wish it to be otherwise? It is as it should be; for science, given that it be open-minded intelligent science, must proceed step by step; and so proceeding, each step, each 'footfall', is and must be consolidated before the scientist can venture reasonably and rationally to take another. Therefore, if the scientist still is not forced to recognise and to learn the reality of the all-permeating spirit in the very work which he himself is undertaking, I have no quarrel with his attitude, none. For had he about a hundred years ago, not denied the possibility of God, he would not (in, I know not how many years from now) have found himself upon the solid ground upon which he *shall* find himself in *asserting* the existence of God.

For, when your scientist, your open-minded reasonable scientist, shall have arrived – by sheer force of his own logical investigations – at the final conclusion that there is, apparent and evident in operation in your mundane earth, in the world about you – the 'cosmos' – when he shall have arrived at an appreciation that there is an intelligence, which is not embodied as you are at the moment, then he will have arrived at that conclusion by slow stages, by steady steps, each of which has been fully reinforced and is capable of being stood firmly upon, and he cannot, he will not, then be able to deny the results of his own work, and therefore his assertion of God, his assertion of spirit and of spirit power will be of infinitely more value than had he, one hundred years ago, assented to the proposition whilst knowing nothing of it. That is the purpose, that is the final purpose.

Questioner. The thing that troubles me at the present time is the apparent spirit of antagonism not only in the scientific mind but in the mind of the layman; He is willing to accept all kinds of abstruse scientific statements, whether he knows anything about them or not, but mention 'survival' and a spirit of antagonism promptly arises which is difficult to overcome. We who have accepted these things find it very difficult to understand, although I will admit that I myself possibly twenty years ago would have scoffed in the same way that many people do today.

Abu. I thank you, but I would venture to draw a distinction between the man in the street to whom you have referred and the scientist of whom we have been speaking, for it is not to be expected that the man in the street shall be scientist as well as all else that he is. It is not possible for him to concentrate his attention upon such matters, be they religious, be they scientific, or be they spiritualistic; he has, in short, his life to live; it is an immediacy, and immediacies are always before you; they are your biggest 'handicap' of course. And therefore the man in the street, whilst living his life, has necessarily to be prepared largely to base his religion upon what he is offered by the church, if he can swallow it; to accept his science based upon what he is offered by those who specialise – by the scientists; and neither of those offerings to the man in the street at the present moment carry with them any direct implication of the survival of the spirit of man, or of communication – of 'spiritualism' in short.

But they will do so, even the churches, but before the churches the scientists,

13

for the church will lag behind because it is a vested interest. I digress for a moment to remark that it is nothing to the scientist, it matters *not* whether he discovers, whether he finds upon his own terms that man survives death, or whether he finds on his own terms that man does not survive death, it is nothing to the *scientist*. But it is everything to the orthodox person who is endeavouring to conduct this religious creed, this religious code, which has been rammed into the people for so long, for thereby hangs the whole of the organisation. And now to my theme – I was speaking of the man in the street. When the scientist shall find himself compelled to announce, as he will find himself compelled to announce, that what we, you and I, know as spirit, all-permeating spirit, (the scientist may give it another name, he may call it an ether), the scientist may find that there is what he may call an ether and that this ether, as will be discovered scientifically, appears to be imbued with what you know as intelligence.

That is the great step that science has to make, to find that the world, the very material world upon which you dwell, is not a dead thing but that its very *matter* is permeated with intelligence, with spirit intelligence, with an 'ether'. And when your scientist shall, bluntly and heedless of the results, announce to the world that this is so, the man in the street, after a suitable lapse of time whilst he is being very doubtful upon the point, the man in the street will accept the 'intelligent ether', the God, the Spirit, just as he has accepted your various machines, which have made nothing of time and space even upon your world. And then, and not until then – will the church awaken from its dreadful slumber and will say to mankind:- "But this is what we have been telling you for two thousand years." I leave the judgement in your hands and in the hands of those shall follow you, for we know that it is not so. Regrettably those who should have led have been sadly lagging at the rear.

That expedition is desirable I will agree; whilst not being impatient upon the matter, I would feel extremely regretful if the process of enlightening mankind should be allowed to lag for want of effort on our part, on my part, or upon your part. How then you will ask, how then can you assist in the matter?

And that, is just exactly what I, quite some little time ago in terms of your earthly months and years, asked myself in the plane, the sphere, call it what you will, in which I have my being normally. I metaphorically 'scratched my head' (that is an earthly expression) and I thought to myself, what can I do? Signs and wonders they have had; it might be that I could produce signs and wonders, but it would but be 'another one', and it has been said that though one rise from the dead yet still they will not believe. And so I concluded that such small talent as I might possess in stringing together words which shall endeavour to convey something of the ideas which were in my mind – which are founded upon experience and upon reason and upon love – that I could exercise such talent as I might possess, in speaking aloud, through the use of an instrument kindly loaned to me for the purpose, to at least *one* dweller upon earth. What a little thing, what a foolish thing, for a high spirit teacher to do under the impression that he is achieving anything at all!

This situation is multiplied a thousandfold in your own country and elsewhere in your world. Please, please, do not imagine that the little pool in which we now play is the whole ocean, nor, please, will you feel – I ask it that you shall not feel – that the ocean of mankind is so vast that no little stone that *you* may cast in can make any difference. But you are not alone in casting the stones, there are many, many others. Should you refrain from casting your stone then a portion of this placid lake of incredulity, of stupidity, might remain undisturbed where you could have disturbed it, and that were a pity. That is the purpose of my appearance among you.

Chapter Three

SELF-REALISATION. SIN, GUILT AND ATONEMENT

Questioner. A lady in our circle has been reflecting on questions which have been life-long ideas with her as with many other people – the things which have been called 'Sin' and 'Guilt', and the associated idea of what is called 'Atonement'. We have suggested, after listening to teaching from you that any 'Atonement' must in some sense come from or through oneself after viewing the supposed Sin and Guilt. She does not find that, as yet, a satisfying answer. Will you please try to give us some clearer ideas on this subject?

Abu. I would, by way of preamble, before dealing with your question, refer you to a phrase which was made use of in your little opening address to *us*, in which it was stated that one of the purposes of your meeting here together, in harmony among yourselves and in harmony with those of the spirit world who are gathered also to meet and greet you – one of the purposes of such meeting was to assist you to come into a relationship with yourselves, and this is a phrase which will bear considerable examination.

I would venture to say without unkindness that the majority of mankind, even particularly of educated mankind, is in fact in no sense really in a true relationship with itself, largely because the open, naked and unashamed relationship which man should have with his own being, his own 'ego', if you will allow the word, is smothered, is overlaid by accretions, by ideas and by notions, which have slowly grown up over the course of centuries and which have become apparently part of what one may call man's second nature.

And, for no good reason, for there is no reason at all, but for no *good* reason, man has generally refused to enter into a true relationship with himself. That is why I say that the phrase which you used was a pregnant phrase and will bear considerable examination, because it is a vital matter, when considering the subject of sin, of guilt and of the possibility of atonement. I will come to those words a little later. But a true, naked and unashamed realisation of man's relationship with himself, which is a phrase which might be held to be without meaning by some who do not think upon it, is a phrase which really means the relationship of the conscious thinking part of the mind of man with the greater part of the mind of man, of which he is not, whilst incarnate, conscious. That is the relationship which is vitally important, and if a man shall arrive at a happy and a fortunate and a harmonious relationship between the conscious and the 'subconscious' facets of his mind, then that man will be at peace within himself, and sin, the concept of sin, will not have weight with him and he will feel no guilt, because the process of self-realisation, which is the realisation of that relationship, will have been a mutual one.

For the conscious mind cannot delve into the subconscious mind and endeavour to arrive at an appreciation thereof and a relationship thereto without the converse process taking place of an outflowing from the subconscious part of the mind into the conscious part. And so for such a one, the subject of sin holds little difficulty. That would appear to sweep the project away ruthlessly and without regard to the difficulties and the troubles which my sister may be experiencing within her own conscious thinking mind, and perhaps that of others of you also, but I would not wish that it were so. I merely make the point simply because you did make use of that phrase and it is a valuable and a useful one.

This process of self-realisation is not a simple one, for the reasons, (which are no *reasons* at all) which I have already given you, namely that the conscious, thinking part of the mind of man has become cluttered up, if I may use such a word, with débris, with rubbish in many cases, which inhibits the very process of self-realisation, and it is necessary for a man, before he can come to grips with himself, to throw away a great deal of the lumber with which the conscious mind is necessarily cluttered. Necessarily, because of the accident of birth in place and in time, which carries with it these things, (the lumber of which I speak,) and it is a difficult process to commence consciously, because the conscious mind has apparently no external standard by which to judge which of its contents are lumber and which are of value.

And now I will leave my hypothetically ideal man who has achieved self-realisation and has come to terms with himself without, please note, without rejecting *all* the content of his conscious mind and calling it "illusion"; that is not the way to arrive at a self-realisation, for that way results finally in a dismissal of the *self* as yet another illusion, and leaves the man in a very similar position to that in which he was before he commenced the operation. However, we will let that pass for now and will come down to the apparently more simple topic of 'sin'.

My sister has also used the word 'guilt', and I would wish to define, if I may, these two words, in order that we may be quite clear of what I am speaking. Sin then is to be regarded as the offence, be it of omission or of commission, the offence, (it is not stated against whom) and guilt as the feeling which follows upon such 'sinning'; will you accept that definition? Then we can discuss the matter of sin and realise that it includes the subsequent *feeling* of guilt. The question of atonement will necessarily appear a little later.

Now sin. Sin, as I have said, implies an offence, of commission or omission; "We have done those things that we ought not to have done and we have left undone those things that we ought to have done", is that not the phrase? But to whom, against whom, is the offence committed? If it is an offence against the earthly laws of the country in which you happen to dwell it is not necessarily to be regarded as sinful; it may be a crime and it will be punished, if it shall come to light, by earthly justice, and if earthly justice is satisfied the crime is expiated, but that is not necessarily sin. Then, against one's fellowmen? Yes, perhaps, for sin *can* be committed against one's fellowman where no *crime* is committed, and it will of course be well within the knowledge and the understanding of all of you that it is possible by backbiting – by many, many ways – to offend against your brother or your sister without committing any offence against the laws of the land. There, my 'yardstick' – the only yardstick – should of course be brought to bear, before the offence is committed – necessarily. Is this thing such as I would wish to have my brother do to me or is it otherwise? If it is otherwise then it must be placed under the heading of an offence and therefore, if you insist upon the ugly little word, of a 'sin'.

Very well, that would dispose of the question of sin, for you can commit offences, sins that is to say, against your fellow-beings, and you are warded

17

against so doing (in so far as you are able to follow the signpost) by recognising this signpost of love; Love one another, do unto others as you would that they should do unto you; in so far as you can recognise that, you are armed against such sins. Very well. Then, sin against yourself. Yes, that is possible, that is quite possible, but if no other person, no other soul, no other spirit, shall suffer because of your sin against yourself, whatever its nature may be (and I would prefer not to go into details on that particular point), if no other person, I say, shall suffer therefrom, then it is a matter for yourself. If you wish to offend against yourself, you are welcome so to do, for it is you who will pay; If you shall indulge unduly in – I do not know – in earthly things, possibly so simple a matter as overeating, the result will be apparent to yourself and so you will automatically suffer for your sin against yourself.

That is to say your brother has been taken care of and you yourself have been taken care of, and now we come to the sin against God; and there I lower my voice, for it is surely of the utmost importance, it is surely a vital matter, a matter which shall make man – the spirit of man – tremble to its foundations with fear that he may offend by sinning against the mighty God: Need I be more sarcastic in my tone?

My children, it may be difficult for some of you to accede to the words that I am about to use, but I say clearly to you now that you *cannot* sin against God. You can sin against your fellowman and that is not pleasing in the sight of your Father, for He is the Father of your brother as well as the Father of yourself – it is not pleasing. You may sin against yourself and that is foolishness rather then sin. But sin against your loving Father you cannot do, for sin would imply that He will arise in His wrath and will be offended. I have used already the word 'offence' as a substitute for sin, and an offence implies an offended one, and so you cannot sin or offend against your Father God. You may cause him to weep perhaps, but to make Him arise in wrath, to offend against Him, no, it cannot be. It is hardly reasonable for me to endeavour to give you reasons for such a statement, for it is quite evident that the statement transcends reason itself, but I will make this one point: that the love of your Father, your Father God, is as far above and beyond any concept of love that you can possibly have at your present stage of spiritual evolution as is His understanding beyond even the understanding which you may have between yourselves and your fellowmen. And with love such as that and understanding such as that you cannot offend.

You will not, bethink yourself, that your Father God, the great spirit – I cannot find words to indicate our concept of God:- we cannot and must not conceive of Him as a petty, a paltry personage, whose ear is pricked to listen to the syllables of a word which is not used perhaps in your polite society and thereupon to be offended thereby. Indeed, indeed, no, that would be a lack of understanding, for your Father cannot only see into your heart, your Father is a part thereof. The hearts of all of you are a part *of* the Father, and how could He lack complete understanding of what is in the heart of each and every one of you, since that heart of yours is a part of this Father God, of whom we speak and whom we love, because when we love *anything* or anybody we are necessarily loving God, who is all love. And so I say, without fear of contradiction, for I do not mind if I am contradicted, that you cannot sin against God in any sense which would indicate that God is offended with you. Very well, then, that dismisses the question of sin against the Father.

Now we will come again to the question of sin against your fellowman, for I have disposed, I think, of sin against yourself as little more than foolishness. So there remains then nothing that is of importance to consider except a sin – an offence, that is to say – against your fellow being; human and non-human alike. You can offend, as I have admitted, against them – you may be guided not so to offend by the use of the yardstick of love, or you may ignore that, perhaps in haste, in anger, or in sheer ignorance, and offence may be committed. Later a realisation that an offence has been committed may bring upon the sinner the feeling which we know as guilt, and we have agreed to accept that as a corollary of the realisation of sin, of offence. Very well. You have offended against your brother and you have suffered thereafter the feeling of guilt, which is a realisation that you have so offended. Then you shall go and correct the matter, you shall put it right, if it can be done. You shall take the hand of your brother and you shall explain the circumstances, and you shall put right whatever may be put right in worldly terms, and you shall expiate your sin thus by nullifying its effects. But perhaps it cannot be done, or, my children, and I speak in all seriousness now, it may be that it *could* be done but that pride, position, or something of an earthly nature withholds you from so doing, (I am speaking as it were to the whole of mankind, and not of course to any one individual); if then these worldly things shall withhold a man from rectifying a matter which he has realised is wrong and which could be rectified, the sin, the offence, and necessarily the feeling of guilt thereupon, must remain with him.

And sooner or later the spirit of that man will depart from the plane of earth and the opportunity of rectifying the offence will then apparently be lost, and indeed may be lost for a time, and the man will then – the spirit of the man – suffer from this feeling of guilt and remorse and a full realisation of the fact that he has offended against his brother man, that he could have put the matter right but had failed to do so, and that now he is in a position where he cannot apparently put the matter right; The sin will be expiated thus, it will be purged and burned out in the fire of remorse – which, you will complain, does not aid or assist the man who was offended against. That is very true, but you must take a broader view; you must not think that because one during his earthly life has been greatly offend against by his fellowmen he is therefore to suffer in a future existence, for it is not so. There will not be a 'recompense' for his sufferings, in the sense that the more he has suffered the more glorious a habitation he shall have when he passes to the spirit plane, no, that is not so, because it is his own life which shall make the conditions which he shall inhabit, and what he may have suffered will not necessarily bring a 'reward', for suffering cannot be paid for in gold nor can it be paid for in conditions; but it does not greatly matter.

I had occasion a little while ago to refer you, apropos something else, to your school days when you have been caned for an offence of some kind, and I reminded you that that caning no longer rankled within your minds; and correspondingly this hypothetical person, who has been greatly offended against, will not hold a grudge against life, against his fellowman, against God; when he shall have passed to the spirit sphere and shall have oriented himself, according to his own life, upon that sphere, he will no longer be offended. It is the one who has *caused* the offence who will suffer, and he will suffer because he himself will be brought to the realisation of what he has done and what he could have undone, and remorse and sadness of spirit will be his lot for a time, and thus will his sin, his offence, against his fellowman be expiated.

That is not atonement. For atonement would suggest reparation, and in this particular case reparation could not be made, so it is not atonement. If and where an offence can be atoned for by the making up to the injured party in some way, then the offence is rendered null and void and is of no importance and has no effect upon either party.

And now, if you please, I will have further questioning, for I am sure I have left a number of loose ends . . .

Questioner. I think that is very plain, and I thank you.

Abu. Then perhaps I should round off what I have said. I think I must finally touch upon this matter of atonement, if only because certain religious schemes in your world have offered various suggestions of a vicarious atonement – that one man may suffer and may take upon himself the burden of sin for another or other men. That I reject utterly, utterly and completely. It does not matter who the man may be, how willing he may be to suffer for another, it may not be done.

There is no vicarious atonement. Your Father God demands no reparation, demands no atonement, for, as I have told you, you do not sin against Him, for He understands, and though you shall set yourself, deliberately, wittingly and intentionally, to insult and to offend against your Father God to the greatest of your ability, His smile will continue. It will be a pitying smile, He will not be cross, He will not arise in wrath; you have not offended against your Father God, for He understands and He loves. More than that I cannot say.

Questioner. I think I have one question. What about those who just deny the existence of God, who do not feel the loving arms of God, and are just not prepared to accept Him? Whatever they do, however they think, God does not exist for them, they are not prepared to accept God. How does God look upon those children?

Abu. How would you expect the Father to look upon this erring or errant child? Would you expect him to be cross and to be annoyed because His majesty, His Fatherhood, are not recognised by this child?

Questioner. But I think it is just this and this only which I would call sin.

Abu. To sin against God by denying Him? My child, I must use a little simile. If your barndoor fowls who are penned and kept by human beings shall take it upon themselves to deny the existence of such human beings, are the human beings thereby affected? Not in the least.

Questioner. This question is rather vital to me, for I must tell you that I myself, not so very long ago, was in a state when I denied the existence of God. I found my way to God only gradually and slowly – with his help, yes – but ever since then I feel terribly guilty that I should ever have got into a state like that, and that

Abu. My child, if you are wishing to suggest that I shall accept your words as indicating that because you have a feeling of guilt therefore you committed a sin, I will not so be drawn, for that is not the case. Your feeling of guilt is a feeling within yourself, and now that you have admitted that you have arrived again knowingly under the hand of the loving Father you should endeavour to throw from you, to cast from you, that feeling of guilt, for it never was warranted, and it is even less warranted now.

I will venture to quote again: "There is more joy in heaven over one sinner that repenteth than over ninety and nine just persons who need no repentance"; and so my child, if you have had or still have a feeling that in the past you have sinned and therefore you feel guilty about that, now that you have, if I may use the words "returned to the fold" (they are quite meaningless for indeed you have never strayed from the fold) – then you should rejoice that you have found your way back; for it is you who have come back to the Father, not He who ever left you. Though you deny your God He will not deny you. There is no sin in what you have told me, my child, and I wish with all my heart that I could assist in dispelling the feeling of guilt, for the only feeling which your loving and understanding Father would find within Himself in such circumstances would be one of overwhelming joy that you no longer need to feel a sense of guilt.

I have listened about your world, I have heard comment on many sides referring to schemes of religion, and I have heard comment of various kinds, to the favouring or the disfavouring of one set of beliefs or of another set of beliefs, and I have told you myself that in my view it does not matter which set of beliefs you shall hold. You cannot *worship* a wrong God, a false God, for there is none such; there is but one God, and so, whether you worship at all or not, whether you even recognise your sonship to the Father God is immaterial. At this present stage of existence it is understandable that there should be confusion among you, as indeed there is; it will be resolved, and no sin of which you may deem yourselves capable – and I would administer a mild reprimand to mankind in general in this respect, that he does tend to set himself a little upon a pedestal in the matter of sinning, appearing to think that he is of such vital importance that he can offend against his mighty Father – he is not so powerful, though that is not my reason for saying that you cannot sin against God. But it is not material whether you subscribe to a certain creed, or to none, it does not matter; and in the spirit sphere to which you must all eventually go you will be given opportunity to achieve this self-realisation, to come to grips with yourselves, to enter into a true and proper relationship with yourselves, and in so doing you will enter into a proper relationship with God the Father. Further than that I cannot go.

Do not, I beg you, do not place too high a rating of importance upon this earthly existence which you now undergo: your triumphs are petty, that you will admit; your sins are equally so.

With all blessing, I will leave you, and shall as always be happy when I am again given opportunity to discuss these points, these matters of varying interest, of varying importance. Always I disclaim authority, of that you are well and fully aware, but on matters such as those which we have discussed this evening I would not wish you to think that I speak in any way lightly. I speak from an experience of earthlife, I speak from an experience through spirit spheres, I speak from an experience of return to contact with earthly conditions, and I speak of what I *know*. If you shall accept that what I know is the truth in these respects, then am I happy, for my words come to you, as you are well aware, with love and desire to aid and to help the struggling souls and spirits of men and of my children in particular. I do not endeavour to lay down the law, quite the reverse, but on matters which are important, as indeed man's self-realisation is important, I can but pray that I have been guided to use words which shall have meaning for you and which shall perhaps a little assist you to the process of self-realisation of which we have spoken.

Chapter Four

MEDIUMSHIP

Questioner. It is an objection frequently raised when dealing with this whole subject that there should be no necessity for "mediums". Mediumship is a comparatively rare gift and that spiritual or philosophical teaching should apparently depend on the "accident" of making contact with a "medium" is thought by these objectors to throw a kind of "cloud" over the whole business. Can you give me any ideas which I might bring forward when trying to deal with objections of this nature?

Abu. I thank you for the opportunity to speak upon the point. It is going to be a little difficult for me to give you something cast-iron, as you might say, with which you may demolish the objections. The objection to mediumship which you find expressed occasionally is not necessarily a bad thing in itself. But, as you have made the point, how then without a medium – as means, that is to say – how then is the sceptic, the unbeliever – the one who *cannot* accept what he is told – how then is he to be brought to the knowledge of the continuance of life and of the communication between the two worlds, for those are the "matters" which depend upon exterior mediumship?

In point of fact, of course, each and every one among you should be and to some degree is his or her own "medium" in that, to some degree, you are all susceptible to impacts from the spirit-world, but the majority of men and women upon the earth-plane do not appreciate this.

None the less the love of God, of which I have spoken, does make an impact upon them in one way or another and so "mediumship" as such is not really required for *that* particular manifestation. But, it is necessary – it is essential – to establish reasonably, by your ordinary mental processes, the *fact* of the continuance of life and the possibility of communication between the incarnate and discarnate spirits of men.

I can offer you but little – nothing, I fear, of which you have not already knowledge – for your objectors will be fully aware of the necessity for a means (and the word "medium" signifies nothing but a means to an end, of course) – your objectors must be aware of the necessity of a means or a medium of communication upon your earth-plane – a means between themselves, their own wants, and the satisfying of those wants, at every turn.

The objection arises, it would seem to me, from the perhaps somewhat unusual nature – as it would appear to the ordinary man – of the communications which are received, since, when a man is "dead" he is dead and that is the end of it. That is the natural, normal viewpoint, perhaps, for one who has seen the body lowered into the grave and who knows nothing, directly or indirectly, of the spirit activity which persists and continues.

But, should you wish to speak – to communicate the one with the other in the same manner as that which I am now using – there is the means, there is the "medium", there is the atmosphere which conveys the sound – in scientific terms there are vibrations – from the voice of the speaker to the ear of the hearer. Without that means, that link, there would be no speech; all would be silent. The same applies in nearly all your walks of life where any form of communication or communion is necessary as between man and man whilst incarnate, if only because the spirit of man whilst dwelling upon the earth-plane is imprisoned in the limited conditions of the physical plane which require these media – which insist upon these media – in order that communication may be established between mind and mind. It can be done directly only in a very fragmentary way because again of the limitations and because the mind – which is a spirit thing – has become accustomed to the acceptance of the limitations and, in general, is prepared to accept the limited conditions as the natural, the normal and all that there is.

You know otherwise and so does the *soul* of every man but his thinking mind may not know otherwise. At every step some medium must be used for man incarnate to communicate in any way whatsoever with another man incarnate. Why then should there be any objection to the necessity for the use of a medium – a means – in order that man discarnate should communicate with man still incarnate? To me it offers no difficulty and I think that your objectors object, perhaps, not from reason but because they have not *applied* their reason to the matter.

There are the two aspects (I would repeat what I have already said) there are the two aspects – the one being the purely spiritual approach which can be made and is made between the spirit-world and the spirits of men upon earth, dwelling in the body. Of that approach, of that impact, the majority of men, I suppose, are quite unconscious, but they receive it none the less. There is no need for a medium there because, in a case such as that, spirit speaks directly to spirit.

But your objectors raise an objection to the necessity for a medium in order that they may *hear* the voice, that they may *see* the wonders (if wonders can be performed) and they think that these things perhaps should be performed for *their* benefit without the interposition of what appears to them to be a "third party". But there is no third party. The medium which I myself am using at this moment is not the spirit of the man who uses this body. It is the body only – it is the vehicle – there is no third party. I, Abu, am clothed upon for the moment with this physical body which belongs not to me, and the spirit to whom the body rightly belongs is taking no part in the communication. Therefore, in that sense, there is no medium – there is an *instrument* and it is a better word. I, Abu, am able and privileged to make use of an instrument that I may speak directly with you. There is no "medium", in the commonly regarded sense of the word; there is no third party.

Questioner. There is not an "intervener".

Abu. That is the essence. The word "medium" is, perhaps, a little unfortunate and I myself would prefer to use the word "instrument", for such it is, be it body – the vocal chords – or be it a portion of the mind – the brain – of the medium which is being used. They are but instruments for our purposes when we are permitted to communicate with you.

Questioner. I would like to ask a second question which has this connection with my first – that it is an attempt to deal with various "objections" which

I find are raised by critics.

How is it that of all the capable, worthy and intelligent people who come over to your side, there are so few from whom anything is heard again? Is the knowledge of communication general (I will not say universal) amongst the spirits of those who have "died" and, if so, how is it that those who might really have something worth while to say, so seldom come and say it?

Abu. You pose a question which bears upon the character and the personality and the individuality of many, many spirit people. Can I speak for them all? Can I answer your question by saying "such a one does not wish to make a communication; such a one wishes to make a communication but has not found a suitable instrument"? Your question is too wide for a general answer.

The fact is as you have suggested – the *fact* is – that the spirits of all men and women when they come to dwell upon the spirit side of life, are advised, are informed, that they can, in certain circumstances, make communication to those remaining yet upon the earth-plane. That is done, I say without fear of contradiction, in every case. For, since so many men and women pass across this veil and enter into this life with *no* knowledge, with no understanding of the circumstances and the conditions in which they find themselves and in which they *will* find themselves with no preparation, as it were, at all and are frequently greatly distressed and greatly bewildered – the more so, frequently, because they, no longer being bounden and limited by the physical body, are more sensitive – one might almost say, by comparison "hypersensitive" – to the feelings, to the emotions of those whom they loved and love still upon the earth-plane and, therefore, the grief and the distress which are felt, not unnaturally, by those who have been "bereaved", is felt also by the spirit who has stepped forward one pace – just a little before. Therefore, it is necessary that these arrivals should be informed of the facts – should be told of circumstances as they exist – that their own feelings of sadness are not necessarily, or very seldom, due to the circumstances and the conditions in which they find themselves and in which they *will* find themselves, but far more so to a reaction from the grief and the sorrow of those loved ones whom they have necessarily left behind a little while.

And so the newly arrived one is made aware of the possibility of communication, (one-way communication, if you will, for the time being) with the earth-plane and it is explained that they can, given the circumstances, given the desire of those remaining upon earth, make themselves known to their loved ones by the use of the much despised "medium". Otherwise it is a very difficult thing, because always of the limitations of your earthly bodies, for the freed and liberated spirit who would so wish, to enter into the mind and heart of the loved one left behind and to console their grief and to dry their tears by giving assurance of their continued well-being, their continued living, their continued loving. But, it cannot be done directly in many cases . . . sometimes . . . sometimes, yes.

But then, you see, the whole business of communication is not simple. It is a complicated matter; it depends upon a great number of things and so it is not *possible* for the volume of spirit people who would wish to speak to their loved ones so to do frequently. Suitable conditions are not to be found; the loved one does not come into contact with the philosophy that you call "spiritualism";

25

learns and knows nothing of the possibilities of communication with the dear one who has gone on before; even having learned perhaps of this and visiting a "medium" quite blindly – for you have, so far as I am aware, no "yardstick", whereby you can measure the sympathy of the vibrations between the sitter and the instrument and the communicator (all of which are necessary and essential before a real and moving and living communication can be made). So that, the bereaved one may actually seek out a medium only to find that there is no contact or an imperfect contact and not to be aware of the why of this failure. That is the position.

Questioner. I was thinking rather of those minds – the great teachers and preachers – who, in the past centuries must have come to your side in large numbers. How is it that they never seem to return (knowing, as you say, of the possibility) to teach the better truth they may now be aware of or even to undo, if possible, some of the error they were responsible for?

Abu. Two points I must make in response to your objection. The first – do you speak with knowledge?

Questioner. I don't know that I can say that I speak "with knowledge" but I read everything that is to be read; I discuss these things with people to a reasonable extent – I don't know how far I can trust all that.

Abu. The second – a more mundane point but a point of psychological importance. We will instance a teacher – perhaps a great teacher upon the earth-plane who was, perchance, misguided as you have suggested and who would wish, upon his receiving of enlightenment, and learning – as he will certainly learn – wherein he erred, will wish to return to the earth-plane in so far as he can, imperfectly through a medium, in order to rectify – again in so far as he can – such wrongs as he may have taught or errors that he may have expressed. He will wish so to return and we will suppose that he does so return and that he gives his own name and makes himself known to a circle of people such as yourselves. (It is, you will recall a great name, perhaps a world-famous name). There will be those among his hearers who will say: "This is not "X" for "X" taught otherwise".

So, my first question to you: "Do you speak with knowledge?" – it was not fair, for you could not have the knowledge.

But I tell you that teachers who have had influence and who have misled the thoughts and the minds of the people who have listened to them – in error, not wittingly – those teachers do return, those teachers will return, for it is incumbent upon them so to do in order that they may use their every endeavour to rectify the errors which they may have propagated. But, because of my second answer, because of the scepticism which would certainly arise, these teachers infrequently use the name by which they were known.

Therefore, they will then propagate the truth, (I hope – I have no doubt they will propagate the truth as they *find* it), in opposition to the error which they have previously taught but not necessarily using their own names as they were known upon the earth-plane. Thus they may rectify in some measure the wrong which they have done without attempting to seek personal advancement or glorification for themselves therefrom, and that is the important thing – that the feet of the children shall be guided along the true path. It matters not who does the guiding, but if one shall have misled the child, that one may return – anonymously if necessary – in order to bring the child back upon the path.

I think that will answer your difficulty.

"Let your light so shine before men that men may see your good *works* and glorify your Father". It is the *works* – it is not the name, the honour and the glory. You are aware of that.

Chapter Five

INTUITION

Questioner. Could you explain the difference between the ordinary processes of thought and 'intuitive' thought?

Abu. What is the difference between what you know as the ordinary process of thought and what you know as intuition or intuitive thought?

Intuition is not thought at all in the ordinary sense of the word, for the connotations of the word 'thought' are those of a laborious process – of aggregating, of computing, of comparing and of arriving at a conclusion; that is the process of ordinary thought. To handle mentally, as it were, some aspect of a project or thesis which may come within your ken – to handle it piecemeal, to fit the pieces together if they will fit, to endeavour to see eventually at what shape or pattern you shall arrive – that is the ordinary process of thought. You have a long and somewhat ugly word which describes the process – 'ratiocination' – and that is the process which you describe as 'ordinary thought'.

Intuition – intuitive knowledge that is to say – is knowledge arrived at, possibly by personal experience (that is to say, by an immediate impact) or possibly at second hand by an information which shall be presented to you and arrives within your ken (your conscious mind) via and only via what we have agreed to call the 'subconscious' mind – the greater mind. Intuition, in a word, is the thought of the spirit-mind whereas conscious thought is the laborious process of that 'portion' of spirit-mind which is compelled or set aside to deal with the affairs of the physical, material world. And since this 'subconscious' mind is of so much greater capacity (I do not speak in terms of volume or content but of ability) since its capacities are so much greater, it can and does absorb knowledge and information in a manner which can but be described to you as 'intuitively'.

It is a seeing, a seizing upon the resultant without the necessary labour of going around and through all the pieces of the jigsaw puzzle and piecing together the 'resultant' after prolonged effort. You have asked what is the difference between the two processes and of course the short answer is that in intuition there is no *process* as you would understand it at all. For again, as so often, we must touch upon the time-sense and a process such as that of normal thinking, to which you have referred, will necessarily occupy 'time', but intuition does not occupy time: intuition is a timeless apprehension.

Questioner. Is the normal process of thinking assisted?

Abu. The normal process of thinking, my child, is assisted but assisted only by the subconscious mind of the person doing the thinking and not directly. For the spirit-mind of a dweller in spirit (or of a dweller upon earth for that matter) the spirit-mind of such a one cannot (or perhaps very rarely and with great difficulty) *cannot*, generally speaking, make a contact with the portion of mind set aside for dealing with earth affairs – again for the same reason which I have expounded to you, that this 'portion' of mind was originally set aside for a special purpose. Were that conscious mind, as we now know it, susceptible to constant impact from the spirit side of life, it would be unable to give the close attention which it must give to the affairs of the physical world and therefore it is as it were 'shut off' from the spirit world or the spirit life except for the channel between the 'subconscious' and conscious minds, and so the conscious mind, receiving information from the spirit world, will receive it, almost necessarily through the medium of the man's *own* subconscious mind. There is the difficulty with regard to communication between the two worlds. For, in order to make use of a physical instrument, in the manner in which I myself am now doing, it is obviously necessary to use the part of the mind which is set aside for the control and regulation of the physical organism of the medium – you will appreciate that? And to make use of that portion of the conscious mind (albeit at the moment it is in your eyes unconscious) it is necessary to canalise the intentions, the wishes, through the subconscious, the spirit-mind. Which bears out what I have just said, that it is well-nigh impossible or at least very rare and difficult to make a contact with the conscious mind of an earthdweller without passing through that person's subconscious mind. And thereupon, of course, the subconscious mind of the medium may give a twist to the words which are coming through or which are being endeavoured to be passed through. And that process is inescapable.

Questioner. That, I take it, is why people getting this 'information' as you call it, from or through their subconscious minds are so apt to say: "Ah, but this is all my imagination", thinking that, since it comes through their own subconscious mind, they have originated it .

Abu. Precisely. There is an awareness; not in circumstances such as this, for, as you appreciate, the conscious mind of my instrument at the moment is not a conscious mind as far as he is concerned; it is a conscious mind only in so far as *I* am concerned. But, given a case where an instrument shall be functioning perhaps in another mode, where the person concerned remains conscious or in a 'normal' state, then the information handed to the subconscious mind of that medium by helpful friends dwelling in spirit, upon being handed down *to* the conscious mind, will appear to some degree at least as if it were the *product* of his own subconscious mind. And such in fact may be the case; but such in fact may equally *not* be the case. Therein lies, of course, the one big difficulty of communication as at present practised: the impossibility in so far as I myself am aware, of controlling the conscious mind of an instrument without controlling the subconscious mind.

When the conscious mind turns its attention towards the things of the spirit in an endeavour to achieve a communication direct with the spirit, it will naturally and normally project its effort in a 'straight line' and thus fail to arrive at the 'message' – the very place where the message is. That is the picture which you have drawn but a better picture, because more scientific, would I think be this. You are to imagine the earth-plane, that is to say your minds upon the earth-plane, as being of a a certain order of vibration. You are to imagine your subconscious mind, (your spirit-mind) as being of another order of vibration at a higher rate of frequency. When these two shall impinge the one upon the other (or shall be made to impinge) there will be a resultant frequency – a 'heterodyne' I believe is your phrase. When the higher frequency of the spirit-mind shall impact upon the lower frequency of the conscious mind there will be this heterodyne wave and the conscious mind can by examination of that heterodyne wave decide (since it is of course an intelligent mind) what must have been the frequency of the spirit or subconscious wave which has given rise to that heterodyne.

That is the nature of communication; that is why it is imperfect and incomplete, and that is why there are and always will be difficulties, because there are two rates of frequency, of vibration, in question and it is impossible that it should ever be otherwise.

Questioner. Two 'dimensions' might we say?

Abu. Two dimensions, which comes to the same thing. The two cannot be laid side by side and find themselves matching – it will not be – but there will be a *resultant* and from the one side examination can be made and conclusions arrived at as to the probable 'frequency' as it were, of the wave emitted from the other side. And that is the nature of communication.

Questioner. The 'conclusions', I take it, being more or less reliable according to the ability of the conscious mind which examines them?

Abu. More or less reliable according to the ability of the conscious mind *in this particular direction*. But do not lose sight of the fact that the subconscious mind must also analyse what is being handed to it from the earthplane. We upon the spirit-plane are not omniscient. It is often said and said with truth that those upon the spirit world – I myself for that matter – can receive your thought. Yes indeed, but not in the same manner as that in which you are thinking it. We receive, as it were, the resultant of the impact which I have already described and we, if we have the ability and the desire of course, are able to translate that resultant into something resembling your thought, and that is why we will frequently get the idea underlying your thought without being able to get the thought itself precisely.

To revert to the matter of the ease of resolution, the ease of translation; it depends not only upon the attitude of the conscious and/or the subconscious mind – according to the direction of the transmission, but it depends also upon the closeness of the frequencies. For if one shall be so saintly, so 'holy' a man in the very best meaning of the term – so perfect a being that his conscious mind is truly coincidental with his subconscious mind, there will be little difficulty in translation, whereas, if the reverse be the case there will be great difficulty. And since the frequencies, or the rates of frequency, of mankind are as innumerable as the number of human beings itself, you can understand why one person is more 'psychic' than another, why one person is more 'sympathetic' to another than a third and so on, because of the necessity of this form of reconciliation, of translation, of the incident vibrations, the one upon the other. It is not simple; it is not simple.

Too frequently the matter of communication is referred to as if it were a mere question of those in the spirit world 'cocking an ear' or failing to do so, and upon

30

occasion they, loved and loving ones, may even be blamed for 'turning a deaf ear'. Just consider for one moment, the complexity of the operations that must be performed. And your dear ones must *learn* to do this; it is not a mathematical operation, it is not an operation with the hands; it is a mental operation; but it must be learned none the less. The child upon earth must learn to hear words, it must learn what words mean. That is not a mathematical nor a physical operation, it is a mental one; and this matter of communication is of the same order, or a similar order.

But of course, in the spirit-world there are more possibilities than exist upon the more limited earth-plane, if only for the reason that the mind does not *have* to give attention elsewhere, as I have already explained to you, and so persons whom one might have thought unlikely will become adept at communication whilst others whom one would have expected to have been expert will have the greatest dlfficulty.

Questioner. Our feeling, I think, is one of wonder that we get as much as we do.

Abu. It is matter for thankfulness, and since some kind of communication has been going on from time immemorial it is obviously, as I have stated it to be, within the intention of the loving Father that His children shall not *be* entirely separated and shall *know* themselves not to be entirely separated, even though they must dwell upon differing 'dimensions' for a time. But the loving kindness of the Father has left the door a little ajar indeed and we are grateful that it should be so, for only by such means could the vital message be given to man incarnate upon the earth and he should perhaps be persuaded as to what is his better way, from all points of view.

Chapter Six

THE CONTROL OF THE MIND

Questioner. There is some confusion in our thoughts about individuality and the control of 'mind'. We perceive an entity, a something, which can control and direct our minds but which often fails to do so. It can even be aware that the mind is operating in a way that it disapproves of but it is powerless to stop that operation. What is this entity? If one answers – one's spirit – then what is the 'mind'? Is it a kind of mechanism employed by the spirit? And can the mind be developed without the spirit being first developed?

Abu. Yes, to a degree the mind – the conscious mind that is, with which you are aware – is, broadly speaking, a tool for the spirit. The conscious mind, through various centres in the brain, has control over and regulates the functioning of the physical body – of that you will be aware. There are centres within the brain which are acted upon by the mind and through those brain centres the bodily organism itself is controlled in a motor sense. You have stated that you are aware of a mind which functions, and sometimes functions as you would not wish it to do, and yet you – this mysterious 'you' about which you are questioning me – appears to be unable to control it. Is it not parallel with the physical body?

By reason of an injury perhaps, a shortcoming of some sort, for instance a limb which hitherto has behaved itself quite perfectly will suddenly refuse to do so or will behave imperfectly and will not do as you wish. You may possibly have over-indulged in alcohol and whilst desirous of threading a needle you shall find that your hands are trembling and you cannot control them. What then is this body that the mind cannot control? Is it a separate *entity*? No indeed, it is an instrument only and it is slightly faulty. It will be repaired and when put right will function as you wish it to do, always provided that there is no *permanent* injury or shortcoming which cannot be rectified. Given that it is a temporary circumstance, it shall be rectified and the body will then do as the mind is wishful that it should do. And the *mind*, given that there is no injury to that mind, (and such is possible), the mind will then do as the spirit wishes, and that is spiritual evolution.

We have agreed, for ease of handling, to regard this one mind as if it were in fact manifold and we refer to the conscious and the subconscious minds as if they were two though you are aware that they are but aspects or facets of the greater whole, and it is that whole which is "mentipulated" – I thank you for the word – by the spirit. The manner of such mentipulation I am unable to explain to you, for, whilst being aware that I am spirit as you are spirit, I am also aware that I have a spirit body whilst you have both a spirit body and a physical body, and the spirit which is me (as the spirit which is you) will, by operating upon the mind, or minds, be they spirit, etheric, astral or physical, cause those bodies to do largely as we shall desire, but of course it is necessary that the *mind* shall first respond to the urging of the spirit.

The mind however is more than a mere dead and passive instrument, it is an instrument of co-operation, but it has no life of its own. Very well then, the mind, unlike the physical body, is a co-operating instrument, for it partakes to some degree of the nature of both worlds, necessarily so because, whilst the conscious portion is set aside, as we have said before, its function is to be a link between the spirit and the physical and therefore it is a kind of half-way house in that respect, and it must be an active participant – as the physical body is not. The spirit, you will understand, is concerned with spiritual evolution and it will direct the mind, even as the Great Ones endeavour to direct the affairs of your world – that is to say, in broad outline not in fine detail. The mind, and ultimately the brain responding to the mind, will attend to the details of the matter: the spirit will endeavour to influence the mind and will influence it in the desired direction and the mind will translate the urge into detailed action and detailed thought which shall follow upon that urge.

Now, the physical body, as we have agreed, may upon occasion, to some degree, refuse duty and the mind, as a tool, may – again to some degree – refuse the duty imposed upon it by the spirit. We are getting into more and more rarefied fields, of course, as we go further and further in this direction, but the process whilst not identical, is at least parallel. I hope that will give you sufficient to get hold of and may perhaps even answer your question.

Questioner. The only thing that still puzzles us is this: you said that the mind is a sort of 'half-way house' between spirit and body. It is a participating, that is to say a co-operative instrument, but it appears to have a kind of life of its own.

Abu. Of course it appears to have a life of its own for it is the only tool which the spirit of you has been available with which you can know, in an earthly sense, anything at all. And that is the process of 'becoming', the process of individualising, of realising the selfness of the spirit, as opposed to the general 'pool' of spirit from which that individualising portion has sprung. And of course it is the mind which thinks that *it* is the being, that *it* is the man. And whilst it is being operated upon by the spirit it may well be regarded *as* the man, just as the physical body is regarded by the majority of earth-dwellers as the man himself, though in fact it is but the vehicle of manifestation. And the mind which will control the etheric or astral body in due course is again but another vehicle of manifestation *for* the spirit.

But you see, we are getting into tenuous and vaporous regions where before very long words will cease to have any meaning and that is why the mind thinks that it is the whole man, because it has not the capacity to think beyond *itself*; it cannot do that; it uses the word 'spirit', it uses the word 'transcendental', but what can they mean? They can but mean that the very idea transcends the capacity of the mind to grasp it, but the *spirit* will experience whilst being unable to pass to the mind a concrete description of its experience. As for example, when one shall be taken, (as I have told you is the case), upon a visit to high spheres perhaps: the spirit of the person undergoes an experience and, upon its return, (I am forced to use these spatial terms) it is able to make the mind of it aware that it has undergone an experience, but it can refer to it merely as 'transcendental', for it transcends the capacity of the very instrument which is endeavouring to grasp and to handle it.

33

That is the very process of individualisation – that the spirit shall create for itself and evolve, in this process of 'becoming', not only a physical body through which it can manifest upon the earth-plane, not only an etheric or astral body with which it shall manifest upon succeeding planes, but also a *mind*, which shall be for it the in-between tool through which and only through which, it can *make* these bodies, these vehicles of manifestation; and therefore, as the mind is evolved and developed by the urging of the spirit, that is where the participation or co-operation comes in. That mind becomes more aware of itself as such, and the spirit, by that very process, is becoming individualised.

You, upon the earth-plane, are of course upon a lowly rung of this ladder and these matters will become progressively more clear to you as you advance, as you slough off the heavier bodies. I cannot say that you will see the 'purpose' of individualisation other than that which I have endeavoured to offer to you. I do not know the purpose of the earthly life; it is not a penance; it is not intended as a purgatory; it is a process of development and it is part of the general process of development.

Questioner. Which – to use your word – is transcendental as far as we are concerned.

Abu. And as far as I too am concerned. I am happy to have learned as much as I have learned about the process and I am far, far more happy to have learned that – not withstanding all things – this process is a God-sent process; that it is sent in love, with love and by love and through love, though appearances would so very often seem to deny this fact for you, even on succeeding planes; for even on such planes there are many unhappy and unworthy ones who would be prepared to deny that there was any love evident in their evolution. But they will learn better; as indeed I myself have learned.

Questioner. I am a little puzzled about one thing. When one makes a decision of any kind, is it always the same spirit which gives the answer?

Abu. Yes, my sister, for you have but one, for you are but one spirit.

Questioner. Every now and again you do something and yet, within yourself, you know that it is not wise to do it. Why do you do it? Who decides to do it in spite of the knowledge that it is not wise to do it. It looks as if there were two people, one saying "Do this" and another saying "No, I will do that".

Abu. When one shall thrust his hand into a flame so that it be burnt, it is an unwise thing to do for it will cause pain, it will cause mutilation; quite evidently from an earthly point of view it is a foolish thing to do and yet the minds of men have done just that, under an urging which to them was good enough, and therefore the unwise act became a wise and necessary act. I offer you that as a parallel, but do not forget that this mind thing, being a tool or instrument is a participating instrument, and whilst you are but one spirit, you must work – since it is necessary to step down your activities for this very purpose of becoming – through a suitable instrument, a suitable tool. And this mind which you – the spirit of you – is in process of developing, is not perfect, neither is it perfected, though it is in process of being perfected; and therefore there will be shortcomings in *its* action, in response to the urging of your spirit, just as there will be shortcomings in the response of the physical brain to urgings from the mind itself – which stems from *spirit*. There may be: there probably will be, and I think it is this to which you are referring. Not infrequently conflict appears to arise.

Questioner. Between whom, is what I want to know.

Abu. And so, my sister, you will ask me between what pair of antagonists is this conflict! There is none such. There is frequently conflict between opposing points of view of the same mind, though not of the spirit, for the spirit *knows*. I have made the claim that spirit was, is, and will be perfect; its difficulties, the stumblings which it must undergo, are inherent in the process of becoming and they do not affect the diamond in the least; the diamond may be muddied but it is still the perfect diamond. And the spirit of you, no matter what your experience may be, will still remain the spirit of you, as perfect as it was, as it is, as it will be; for it is of God; but it is undergoing experiences, it is getting muddied over, as I have said before, and there will appear to be conflict because the mind which it has been using must necessarily be required to give attention to wordly matters, to matters of self and at the same time to think, if possible, selflessly, altruistically.

Conflict then must arise because this mind instrument is a participating instrument and is not by any means an automaton. I will refer you to your motor-car: it has no mind of its own but I gather that the driver – which is you – may turn to his companion and say: "I don't know what has come over my car today, it will not do a thing." But the motor-car has no mind, no will, no volition or intention of its own; it has a little difficulty, a little shortcoming, a little drawback of some kind – a parallel again perhaps, or an allegory. But the mind of you will necessarily bring forth conflict because that mind has necessarily been evolved and developed to give attention to the well-being of the material parts of you whilst, on the other hand, the spirit of you is desirous of thinking and of behaving in the God-like manner which is its right and its due, and *between these two aspects* there will necessarily be conflict to some degree. But it is not conflict between two spirit personages; it is the mind which in effect is saying "But not so long ago you advised me to do thus and thus, for it was to my good: now you wish me to do this – why? On the last occasion I did that: it was to the hurting of a fellow man, but what of that, it did me some good; now you suggest that I shall do otherwise". And the spirit must gently urge this recalcitrant instrument into the way in which it *should* go.

It is not terribly important, for there is time and it will be worked out. I cannot help taking the long view and you cannot help taking the short. By all means, endeavour to perfect your lives as the spirits of you would wish to perfect your lives upon earth, even as your lives, and our lives, ultimately will be perfect. You will not achieve perfection upon earth, but strive in that direction by all means. But when you shall become aware of shortcomings, do not think; "This is the end of all: I have failed", for you have not failed and you shall not fail, for the spirit of you – the diamond – is not only a diamond but a beacon-light, and you shall

35

follow that light, which is but a part of the great light which shines upon your world and upon all worlds. It is kin to the light which is *you* and I speak literally, for your friends in the spirit world will be aware of you even as lights when they cannot make a closer contact than that with you. And since this light partakes of the nature of the great beacon of all, it will endeavour to blend therewith and you will do well to endeavour to follow it. You will fall by the way, you will stumble, you will make mistakes, but that your spirit is aware that the jewel should be clean so far as is possible is the purpose of your earth existence: more than that you cannot do.

Chapter Seven

MIND: HUMAN AND TRANSCENDENTAL

Questioner. Since all action presupposes intention and all intention presupposes 'Will', may one conceive of the Universe as a manifestation of Will, spreading from an original source through individual channels: and, if so, how far can we conceive of those channels as Minds, of which our human minds are a type?

Abu. It is going to be a little difficult to answer, for how can the one unlearned in such matters see an association, a close relationship, between the block of ice and the water from which it was derived, since the one is so patently a manifestation of a completely different order from the one from which it is suggested the second has arisen?

That is going to be my difficulty in endeavouring to answer your question. I follow the tenor of your opening remarks and suggestions that action appears to imply intention and intention appears to imply will. That is a matter of common experience with you in human terms. Since then you broaden the question and say that within the Universe about you you find *action* which, following the parallel, evidences intention and will, you ask me how far you may ascribe that will to a mind of a nature similar to your own.

And my answer is going to be unsatisfactory in the extreme. For I am going to answer paradoxically to the effect that you may identify that mind or those minds completely with your own and – the paradox – that there is no resemblance whatever between them! You will wish me to enlarge upon that? It is a paradox which appears to need elucidation but how I am to elucidate it in terms which shall have meaning for you I do not know, except perhaps by analogy, as I have already endeavoured to do. For – if I may simplify your question – since you have referred to a mind or minds, I would here pose a question to you.

Have you, in your mind, some notion of the individualised minds, other than that of what of what we will term the 'God mind'? You were thinking perhaps of those whom I have permitted myself to call the 'Great Ones', who in other places are called 'Lords of the Earth' and by other titles which are bestowed on them?

Questioner. Yes, almost certainly I was.

Abu. But the 'Great Ones' are not and never were human beings. They *are* individualised spirit in the sense that they are portions separated from the great ocean of spirit. But how am I to attempt to describe a mind not contained within nor even associated with *form* at all? For a little reflection on your part will insist that your own mind is 'formless', but it is so closely associated with form through what you have known as the etheric and through the material that it must be for you – as almost equally for me – well-nigh impossible to conceive of mind existing in a formless condition. And yet your own reason will tell you that mind as such must necessarily be *formless*, or perhaps a better way of putting it is that it must exist in a form quite unappreciable to you.

Very well then, for the purpose of this little discussion we will dismiss the greater mind – the 'God Mind' – for that is a concept quite transcendental and it would not be possible for me to discuss it except in so far as I might say that the God Mind comprises 'all the mind that there is', which would have little meaning for you because you would immediately wish to define *that* mind in terms of some other mind, and it cannot be done. And so we will confine our remarks to the minds of the 'Great Ones', to the minds of spirit workers, who will, upon occasion, poke a finger into the pie of earth affairs and into the minds of man (a spirit incarnate) upon earth.

The *nature* of the mind in each and every case is identical, though its development may be very different indeed. I must revert to the analogy for I can do no other – the analogy which I have already given you – and I will press it a little further; but to give you an image, a picture which you can image within your mind, is quite impossible, for I cannot limn mind upon canvas and correspondingly you cannot envisage mind within your mind and you will appreciate that fact. If you will recall that the block of ice, the cube of ice, of which we have spoken, is in its essence in its chemical nature, what you know as water (there is a chemical symbol which stands for water and which indicates its composition) – if you will imagine this ice then, to be nothing but that chemical symbol (which in fact it is) and you will imagine the liquid water from which the cube of ice was derived as being equally nothing but this water, and you will imagine the vapour which is visible to you perhaps in the form of cloud as being again nothing but this water, and you will imagine the invisible gas which is steam, into which water is converted when heat is applied as still being nothing but water, you will have a picture, an analogy, and therefore something which your minds can grasp, of the identification of mind with mind and the apparently complete lack of resemblance between the one at the one end of the scale and the one at the other end of the scale.

The analogy can be pressed as you will see to, I think, its furthest physical limits. For the ice cube has form, has shape, has density, has solidity; furthermore it brings to you the effect which you describe as cold. The steam on the other hand (omitting the intermediate phases) has no form – no form at all – it is invisible, and its effect is certainly not cold, I believe! And so you have, at the opposite points of this compass, two manifestations of a thing – a something – which *in essence* are identical. I can offer you nothing further in terms of mind.

Questioner. In addition then to the 'block of ice' there is also mind which can be represented by the 'steam' which I should not recognise as mind, yet which is none the less the mind at the back of those creative or directive powers to which I referred?

Abu. It is 'mind-stuff'; it is the 'chemical symbol' of the water, holding firm and fast and true throughout numerous varying manifestations thereof but identical in nature, and you have grasped my analogy and the answer which I am endeavouring to give you and you will understand why I had to offer you in the first instance an apparent paradox when I stated that the minds to which you were referring were at one and the same time identical with and yet without the least resemblance the one to the other. The paradox, then, is resolved.

Questioner. It would seem that the old idea, so long held, that there were 'angels' had a certain validity.

Abu. It is perhaps a slightly flowery image but it has a validity as you suggest, particularly as the notion of an angel brings with it certain faculties not possessed by man incarnate and therefore the beings designated 'angels' will appear to the mind of man somewhat transcendental in so far as he is concerned. And of course such is the case; for the God-mind from which all of this originates *is* transcendental but only in the sense that the ice cube could not be expected to recognise its 'compeer' in the jet of steam, and yet they are identical. It is a matter of manifestation and of what we have called evolution and, as the ice cube shall be warmed a little by the warmth (and I am becoming artful) by the warmth of love, so that ice cube shall melt its hardness and lose its sharp corners and will turn into a fluid, the more gentle thing which shall be water – that of course upon your translation from the earth plane to the spirit-plane. And there the sun of love, the warmth and the light, shall beat down upon the more fluid substance which is now the spirit "water", as it were, and it shall eventually be transmuted into the vapour – a vapour still perceptible indeed – and this mind shall dwell then upon a yet higher plane. But sooner or later, since the warmth still beats upon me as upon you, that water vapour will disappear from the sight to which it is at present apparent, and I will be, as I shall dare to hope, converted into the purer 'steam' and thus approach closer and closer to the God-mind from which all this has sprung and continues to spring – in essence the same, in manifestation vastly different, but that is of no moment fundamentally. Does my picture appeal to you?

Questioner. I think now that my expression – 'action presupposing intention' seems to call for a little clarification.

Abu. Yes, for a little clarification, indeed. You shall watch a creature, or creatures – perhaps the tiny beasts which attend upon the son of my son – they will be going about their avocation, they will be going hither and thither and doing this and that. You, I submit, will not be aware of their intentions, is that not so? You are not aware at least of their intention in detail, but you are aware of their over-riding intention which is to store their home with the food of which the son of my son will very shortly rob them!

That is their over-riding intent; but the various little things which they shall do by the way would appear to you to have no connection with or relation with this over-riding plan or intention – you can appreciate that. Then, I will offer to you the suggestion that I accepted as implicit in the question, that action implies intent; we need not consider the further point that intent implies will, but it is necessary to look a little more closely into the matter.

Questioner. You have chosen the bees as an illustration. But the bees act by instinct whilst we humans do not act by instinct, we use our minds. Just where do our minds come into the picture? Is it the case that in every action caused through our thinking there is an intent which has to fit into the over-riding plan?

Abu. I think I begin to gather your difficulty, I was about to refer to what you would regard as natural catastrophes – things in the nature of volcanic eruptions, tidal waves and the like perhaps – and to offer you the suggestion that these patent and obvious 'actions' which, following your suggestion, must have some intent, appear to humankind to be of ill intent if any. But the intent underlying such things is only the functioning under the Law. It carries, if I may use the term, no 'emotional' content; there is no intent, in other words, on the part of the God-mind, to injure his creatures. It may chance that injury shall arise but there is no *intent* on His part that such shall happen, but His intent was and is that the Law, the immutable Law, shall continue and shall be carried out, and *that* we cannot question, we can merely observe.

But you have reduced the problem to a smaller field in referring to the acts performed by humankind under the operation of their own minds and you ask if those operations and the subsequent actions are or must be necessarily fitted in with the *greater* intent – that I take to be your question. My answer is definitely – No. There is no plan or intention 'lying above' – you yourself used the word 'over-riding'. There is then no general intent which 'over-rides' or overlies the whole picture with the suggestion perhaps that your own mind, your own intent, should key in as it were with that same over-riding intent, otherwise you would find yourself 'in hot water'. That is not the position at all. There is intent, there is God-intent, that the ice-cube shall be converted eventually into the warming steam – yes; but the bee who shall fall by the wayside or the one who shall turn aside in order perhaps to brush his wings, has not necessarily got to apply his little mind to fall in line with the greater intent. Correspondingly, you are not required to have within the intent of your mind any reference to any greater or over-riding intent, for there is none such in terms of detail.

The intent in such a case is your own intent, or that of any other human being and no other. If that intent shall be consonant with the Law of love – which is the 'over-riding plan' – then it is well for you; if not, it may not be quite so well for you. I can say no more. But that there is any compulsion upon you, any 'moral suasion' shall I say, that you *should* do thus and thus or that you should *not* do thus and thus, I can not say: it is not so.

And now I think I have laid myself *wide* open, have I not?

Questioner. This brings us back to the old problem of free-will within the Law.

Abu. There is indeed direction of human endeavour on the part of those whom I have designated the Great Ones, but it is not a compulsion in detail. It is – what is the word I am looking for? a gentle urging, perhaps. That is the long view, but that aspect of the thing is associated or allied with the overall plan underlying the Law of love in the first instance and so has no reference to the details any more than the manoeuvres of the individual bee has any necessary connection with the over-riding plan of filling the home with food. But that there are spirits, minds, of loving human beings, still existent, still living, still loving and situate close (very close in what you would no doubt call psychological terms) to your earth-plane, is also the fact. And, just as those minds which upon earth would have, when still in the flesh, used their endeavour to advise you, even if possible to direct you, in a manner which would seem to them to be desirable, so they will endeavour still to do. But that has still no reference to an over-riding plan. That is the action of the individual bee, and there is no direction or compulsion possible from them – only an influencing which will indeed be exercised, just as they would have exercised it had they been still confined in the flesh.

I do not wish that you should confuse the limited, though very well meant, intention, desires and influencing of those of your dear ones close to you because close to the earth, with the intentions, desires and influencing of the Great Ones, who are not even aware of *you* as an individual, any more than you can refer to an individual bee by his christian name!

But the children, both incarnate and discarnate, have a large measure of free-will in spiritual matters and of course an influence which is not intended for the good can also be exercised. That is not to say that the children are mere pawns to be bandied about from an evil spirit to a good one and vice versa – of course not. I merely remark that such is the case: you have evil men upon earth and you have evil spirits not upon earth and just as the good spirits will endeavour to influence you so may the bad spirits endeavour to influence you; but you are guarded and shielded in so far as may be, unless you shall lay yourselves 'open to the attack' or the influence of the bad spirit. I would prefer not to go more deeply into that, for it is a side issue, although an important one.

Questioner. We thank you for your patience with our mental struggles.

Abu. One who lives in a timeless world does not need to have patience: the patience is yours. It were wise to endeavour to realise that there are two points of view – they are not opposing for you are looking in the same direction all the time – but there is the view which is a close-up and there is the view of the distance, and whilst you are having regard to earthly happenings or to happenings immediately succeeding your experiences upon earth, your focus is and must be short and you will see in detail. You will see for example, the individual bee (since I have permitted myself to discourse upon these little creatures) you will see the individual bee and if you shall consider this individual bee as during earth dwelling you must necessarily consider yourselves, you shall say: What an appalling tragedy! What a dreadful thing! This poor bee has gotten his wings wet with rain; he can no longer fly and he is starving. Some well-disposed person may arrive and may present this unhappy bee with a morsel of acceptable food and the bee, after a little, may recover his strength and fly on to continue his work in conjunction with the other bees.

It may well happen, alternatively, that the individual bee may die and cease to take any further part in the operation of the hive. Very well, the same thing applies now. To that individual bee, the fact that his wings are wet and that he can no longer fly is the greatest of tragedies, for he has the urge to continue with his work in the hive, necessarily, quite apart from any feelings that he may have – (I do not know if the individual bee even enjoys or suffers from feelings) – but he will have an urge to continue with the work and so it is a tragedy that he shall die.

Correspondingly with the children upon earth, it is a tragedy that one of the children should *die* for he or she no longer takes his due part in conducting the affairs of his fellows around him. He passes to another sphere where he will again take up work (not necessarily the same work but almost certainly work of the

41

same nature for therein lies his interest) he will again take up work of equal importance and there is then no tragedy for him. The tragedy is only for those who are not aware that the dead one is arisen. But unfocus your eyes from this close, short view and focus them into the distance. You are looking in the same direction and there you see the 'sunlit mountains' whereon dwell, if you will, the 'Great Ones' (since we are endeavouring to deal with personalities this evening) but you cannot see *them;* they are at too vast a distance; you cannot even see any detail of the 'mountains' which form their home (or hive!) for it is at too great a distance. Yet they are affecting you and you are affecting them, but in the greater, wider sense, in the same sense that you are affecting God our Father and He is affecting you; not in the immediate details – they are not important.

We recently had a discussion on the topic of suicide – the endeavour of a human being to cut short his span of existence – in general he is under the impression that he is about to close the book and not just the chapter, for he quite frequently does not know that the book continues. It is a tragic circumstance; it is an appalling tragedy for so many who are associated with this one who shall "suicide". But are not your eyes turned a little too closely to earth? For it is not the end of the story, that is the point. There will, admittedly, be spiritual repercussions, most certainly. When the bee's wings are wet he will fall to the ground and can no longer fly and it is a tragic circumstance. But that is not the end of the book.

A little later and the arisen one shall be arisen, whether he shall have passed from the earth-plane to the plane of spirit by his own hand or by some other means; finally and fundamentally it shall matter not. That is not to say that I 'approve of' suicide!

Questioner. It seems that, by taking the 'short' view, we make ourselves too important?

Abu. My child, you strike, I think, the nail quite firmly upon the head there without a doubt. It is not to be conceived, as I have told my children in the past, that the Father who is love and who is nothing *but* love shall condemn one of the children utterly, whatever that child may do. I have said in the past that you cannot sin against God in the sense that you cannot *offend* God, and if the act known as suicide shall appear to some of the earth-dwellers to be the overwhelming calamity the one sin that cannot be pardoned, then I would wish that my children would shake their heads and clear away the fog from their eyes, for that is not compatible with a Father who is love. It is not so. For a little, yes; for a little while the child may blunder into sorrow, into suffering – for a little while – and it is not desirable that the child should do so and therefore I and others are endeavouring to bring the message to other children so that they may be protected against themselves perhaps, that in their foolishness and their blindness they do not blunder into distress and into suffering which could be avoided. But it is not to be suggested and I will not admit for one moment that it *shall* be suggested, that there is a sin which cannot be pardoned, for no such question arises.

Think of the bee and his hive. The son of my son will collect his little family of bees and he will 'tuck' them up into their little beds and he will not even be aware if two or three have fallen by the wayside. The Father who is love *is* so *aware* but it matters as little in the long run as does the absence of one or two of the little creatures from the hive. The over-all plan will continue and all of the children shall be gathered in. If they shall fall by the wayside and besmirch themselves a little or burn their fingers perhaps, it is matter for sadness but temporary sadness only. And, as my child has said, the eyes too closely held upon the earth-plane and upon the human beings wandering upon its surface do tend to give perhaps a little undue importance to this particular and not very important phase of the existence of your spirits, which shall transcend all this and rise superior, to bask in the warmth and the light of the love which even now are there.

Chapter Eight

THE EMOTIONS

Questioner. The emotions appear to be of a different order from the thinking processes. Their range is very great and we are apt to think of them as 'good' or 'bad'. What is their source and are they an expression of the basic spirit through other channels than the intellectual, 'conscious' mind?

Abu. Their source is the source of all things and your question is shortly answered by yourself. Yes, they are an expression of the basic love, for the emotions as you experience them upon earth (this is going to be a little difficult for you to comprehend) are *all* facets of the one emotion, the emotion of love, the great emotion.

Because, when I have claimed that God is Love and that love is all, I have said what I must say – that love is all. The emotion which you will regard as 'hatred' for example is the obverse of the love emotion in the first instance. I do not wish to deal with the emotions individually unless you would wish me to do so. It would be a lengthy process and I would prefer to speak a little more generally. But the emotion of hatred which is usually directed towards some other is first and foremost an expression of intense self-love. I will not go into that but will leave you to consider the point at your leisure. I think that you will find you will come to agree with me and, if, you disagree, I shall be happy on another occasion to listen to your disagreement. But I think you will find that if one person shall have hatred towards another it is because of a more intense love of self which appears in that guise. For the hatred may be associated with a fear, for example, and fear is again quite evidently an expression of self-love since it is fear for the self or for some one other whom the self may love.

You will find that your emotions – and I include an appreciation of beauty as one of the emotions – can in very general terms and perhaps a little laboriously, all be related either directly or 'obversely' to the one great emotion which is Love and which, in its essence and in its light and its dark aspects will comprise all the emotions to which you are subject upon earth.

The emotions as such, as you have stated, differ from the processes of thought and necessarily so, because the processes of thought, as we have already concluded in earlier talks, are earthly developments. Thought was developed by man for a specific purpose of which we have already spoken. It is a 'man-developed' thing, guided, aided, inspired, influenced, most certainly, but developed by man – that is to say the spirit of man, of course. But his emotions are not developed: they are I suppose you would use the word 'instinctive', and they are instinctive in the strongest sense of the word. And, just because perhaps animals which human beings may regard as lower in the order of creation than themselves do not appear to evince emotion in the same sense and as strongly as emotions are evinced by humankind, this merely means that the human being has developed his 'sensibility' towards and in respect of emotion, for the original impulse which we call emotion has the same source and the same bearing.

Questioner. I am puzzling for the moment over this matter of the 'sensibility'.

44

Does that introduce a new factor, so to speak, into the question?

Abu. It introduces, not a new factor, but an evolution of existent factors. This will lead me into devious paths and we shall have to leave the question of the emotions: it were preferable to reserve it for another occasion. But in fact man, in developing his powers of thinking, his conscious mind and the brain with which the conscious mind shall work, has laid himself open, as it were, to keener appreciation of impacts than was possible before man had developed or evolved these thinking powers of his and so it is rather a different emphasis than a different factor. But I would prefer to elaborate upon the points which we have left only touched upon on a later occasion, if it shall please you. Does what I have said give you something of an understanding?

Questioner. I think your words "something of an understanding" are a fairly good estimate of the situation.

Abu. I would find it – as I have had occasion, not infrequently, to say in the past – I would find it difficult if not impossible to give you a full and true appreciation of this matter, for the emotions of which man is aware during his life upon earth continue, enhanced, in the next phase of his existence. And his powers of thought are similarly enlarged, but they will be directed somewhat differently after a sojourn of a certain time (a certain period) upon the spirit plane of life. The powers of thought will be directed somewhat differently because they will not have to be directed to the matter of a physical universe and consequently the power of thought will extend and will be enhanced, but in a somewhat different 'direction'. Correspondingly, the emotions too will themselves become enhanced, they will be felt the more keenly because they are spirit-attributes in themselves and not physical attributes and, therefore, with no physical body to hinder them, the emotions will be the more powerful upon the spirit. And that process will continue, with the emotional aspect and the intellectual aspect upon converging lines until (and here is why it is impossible for me to give you a full appreciation of the situation) until, in that remoteness, that vastness of distance, of time and space – non-existent time and non-existent space! – which we have agreed to name God, there is *all* emotion, for God is Love; there is *all* comprehension, for God is all intellect; there is all that there is, comprised and combined in the one 'ray' which I have referred to as the 'Love of God'.

For that includes and comprehends the intellect: it has been subjected to a 'bending' process, perhaps, but the power of the intellect, the power of thought, is not *shed*, is not lost, is not thrown away as of no value at any particular stage; it is merely 'bent' a little as it were, in direction, and eventually, the emotions which will in the course of time again transmute themselves into an appreciation of love (in its positive aspect of course), together with the intellect, will find themselves upon converging paths and will ultimately converge into all-loving and all-comprehending 'God-head'. It is a mystical concept but I can do no better. I hope that it will not confuse you more than before.

Questioner. I am puzzling over the 'obverse' aspects of the emotions. How should they be controlled? By the intellect? Is that the way to train them towards an upward path? Obviously one goes down if one does not get rid of this 'obverse' side from one's nature.

Abu. My sister, I do not think I have ever dared to tell my children what they *ought* to do and I will not venture so to do at this point. The yardstick is that of love and all my children have at some time or other been aware of the emotion of love, directed towards some other person – possibly even towards old Abu! Then, as to the effect upon the mind, you rightly suggest, my sister, that these emotions will be susceptible of examination by the intellect, but do not ever permit that the intellect shall explain them away and make them as nothing for I would prefer that the reverse were the case. You will recall that we have spoken upon the "Mind and the Heart".

Very well then, when one of my children shall recall the emotion which is recognised as love, in that it is an outflowing of well-feeling, of well-intent, towards some other – if then some other emotion shall enter in, perhaps of envy, of jealously, or some other emotion which is on the 'obverse' side of the medal – then by all means examine that emotion by means of the intellect and compare it with the emotion which your very heart and soul and spirit has recognised as being 'godly', and if you can find, as I have no doubt you will find, that this thing is a little unworthy perhaps in that, as I have already claimed, it stems from a too intense love of self and consideration for self and an insufficient consideration for the other person – the one of whom a child may be envious or jealous – then, if that less worthy emotion can be trodden under, by all means endeavour so to do. For it will be to your own comforting, not alone that you should endeavour to 'polish your medal' as it were, in the sight of God – by no means – but, as you are only too well aware, when you are at one with the world and you feel an outflowing of compassion, of tenderness, of general benevolence, towards your fellowmen, *you* too are happy.

And so it is not self-seeking, for you are giving. You are giving out what you have received, for your own appreciation of the love of your Father shall, if it may, flow out towards your fellow beings and all shall be made the happier therefore, and all the medals will be shining! But I would not wish my sister or any of my children to construe my words into a suggestion that, if one of the children shall find himself or herself unable to perform this process – that the hatred *will* persist – I would not wish you to construe my words into suggesting that that child is unworthy, is in any sense evil or is sinning – by no means. Because the child will be unhappy and that is the payment. We have discussed the matter of 'sin' and it bears upon this thing.

Chapter Nine

WHO OR WHAT 'EXPERIENCES'

Questioner. How is it that we experience what we call unhappiness? Someone might say: "I am very unhappy". What or who is it that is feeling or experiencing that unhappiness, if it is not the spirit?

Abu. It is a very good question, my sister, a very good question indeed. But it probes, I fear, too deeply into the fundamental essence of things, for me to be able to give you a satisfying answer.

Yes, indeed, it is the spirit which is undergoing the experience of happiness, which must undergo the experience of sorrow; indeed and indeed that is so, for quite evidently the various vessels or vehicles of manifestation in themselves are not sentient; apart from the informing spirit they have no life. The physical body, the lowest of the vehicles of manifestation at this stage, when left by the informing spirit and its finer, more tenuous vehicles will disintegrate into the dust from whence it came, and the same thing applies to the other vehicles unless they shall be held together as we have discussed in the past. But in themselves they are not sentient, and therefore you are right in suggesting that it is the spirit itself which experiences the happiness, which experiences the sorrow, which experiences the pleasure or the pain of an earthly existence. But those experiences are again merely a "polishing of the jewel", in the sense of adding to its content; they are not improving its quality, in so far as its fundamental essence is concerned.

And here is where I knew that I would have difficulty, for I am apparently presenting you with a contradictory picture, a picture of a jewel, unassailable and perfect in its essence through all time, and yet a spirit struggling to cleanse itself and to achieve spiritual advancement and progression in order that it may shine forth, as it once did and as it again will. And it may seem that the picture is a contradictory one for I am speaking of the same spirit.

But I must again recall to you my little analogy of the diamond. The diamond in its essence is pure, is perfect, is unaffected, since of its nature, as I gather, it is almost indestructible in earthly terms; it is very hard and cannot readily or easily be damaged, but if it shall be enclosed, for example, within a leathern purse and that leathern purse containing the diamond shall be rubbed in mud or upon stone, then it is quite certain that the leather will be affected thereby, is it not? The diamond also will receive the percussive effects, it will appreciate what is going on, what is happening to the leather envelope – the diamond will appreciate that, but it will not itself suffer therefore. That is as close a picture as I am able to give you of the circumstances.

Questioner. Perhaps it can experience without being affected, though that seems strange.

Abu. That is the contradiction which I find myself forced to offer you; yes, that is so. You will recall, of course, that the spirit of which I have spoken – it is as I have claimed one, since individualised, one spirit and, in its fundamental essence, it is perfect indeed, as it always was and as it always will be – but you will recall, that it is but a "portion" of that spirit which is manifesting upon your earth-plane. That portion is the portion which reacts to earthly happenings and which suffers or enjoys, which finds happiness, which finds sorrow, due to earthly happenings; and the repercussions, the spiritual connotations, of those experiences are passed through into the greater mind, which is itself unaffected by the actual occurrences, the actual happenings but which is enriched and completed by the impacting of the spiritual connotations of such.

Now you can see, why, to some degree, I find myself compelled to take a slightly remote, impersonal view of the ills that flesh is heir to, because even here and now the spirit of each of you is largely not in contact with the earth-world at all directly, but only in an indirect fashion, and that is why I find myself so frequently compelled to say, it is of no great matter, it is not of great importance, it will not last long, it is not fundamental and vital. To the smaller part of your spirit essence which *is* in contact with the earth-world and its experiences, to that portion of the spirit, yes, indeed, these things are vital, they are immediate and they are urgent, and to the conscious mind which has no knowledge of its greater spirit being, which is being affected, by the *spiritual* connotations of the happenings. To the mind which has no knowledge of such a greater being, then, this earth existence is all the existence that there is, and of course it appears then a vital, fundamental and a most important thing. In fact, it is not so. The perfection of the jewel is not affected, it may be regarded as being muddied over by the experiences through which it passes, and if the person in question is wise he will use his endeavour to cleanse the jewel the sooner that it may shine forth in its pristine beauty, but the jewel as such never was affected deleteriously, despite the pains and the pleasures, the happinesses and the sorrows; they are a small part, they have their part to play, yes, indeed, but they are a small part of the existence of the jewel.

Questioner. Without going into elaborate theses and dogmas about the "I within the I" and that sort of thing – many words have been spun round it – I begin to see that that is really only an elaborate and possibly artificial way of saying what you have been saying.

Abu. That is the case, except that I would take slight exception to the repetition of the word "I", since it would appear to suggest a number of entities, as I believe is in fact postulated, a number of more or less separate entities. That I must deny. One entity, (one "ego" is your word?) one "I" only, with attention directed hitherwards and thitherwards, yes, indeed; one entity, affected more or less by various happenings on various planes of existence, but still the one entity throughout. It is as if you, thinking man, with all the possibilities inherent in your brain capacity – for it is quite evidently the capacity of the brain which limits to a large degree the expression of the spirit within, since spirit is again evidently capable of greater manifestation than the physical body in its present state can yet permit – it is as if you, thinking man, with your mind upon some abstruse topic, searching perhaps, the heavens of thought, shall painfully stub your toe against a stone or against a rock, and you are recalled instantly to earth by the pain in your toe. Would you then say that there were two you's, the one who thinks and the

48

one who feels? No indeed, you are aware that this fortuitous impact with a stone has merely recalled your attention from the abstruse topic upon which it was engaged into the matter of a rather painful big toe; but it is still *you*. And there is the position; the whole man, the whole spirit, is inhabiting here and now, numerous realms, numerous spheres, but for the moment the attention is given to the earth-plane – that portion which is manifest upon the earth-plane, the stubbed toe, in fact – and there are your earthly pains and sorrows; they do affect the whole man, yes indeed, but to what degree by comparison with other things; if you will think over that picture your question will answer itself, I am sure.

It would not be kindly of me to endeavour to persuade you to raise your minds from the contemplation of earth and your physical bodies and of all the happenings which must occur and take place within and around you, it would not be kindly, for to do such would be tantamount to requesting you to withdraw from your earth-world, and that I may not do for it is a part of the experience. But if I can be allowed to try and put the matter in perspective for you, then am I more than satisfied, for more than that I dare not attempt to do.

Questioner. I think that is the best help we can have. To take away our pain would not really help us in the same way, I think.

Abu. Had the spirit not taken the trouble to become manifest at all it would have avoided a great deal of pain and sorrow and distress, but it would have lacked also the heights to which it can rise, and those two, it will be found (in the essence of spirit, not necessarily in each individual, but in the essence of spirit) those two aspects will be found closely to balance the one with the other. Whilst having the deepest of sympathy with the children of earth, in that they must suffer, at the same time I am glad that they must suffer a little because only if they can suffer can they find heights of happiness which are yet possible.

Chapter Ten

"DR. JEKYLL" AND "MR. HYDE"

Questioner. You spoke, in a recent talk, of 'spiritual advancement' as being essentially the concord of Spirit and Mind. I found that a most enlightening idea and should be glad if you could add anything to your words on that point.

Abu. And how happy I should be if there were more that I could add, but unless you shall question me specifically, I feel that by your own phrasing of the words you have used you have sufficiently grasped the position as it exists, and since, in order to speak of this matter of concord – an excellent word – I must refer to Spirit, which I cannot define for you, it is going to be very difficult for me to say more than I have said upon the point.

*Questioner. In another talk bearing on the same matter, when we questioned you as to the two minds supposedly in conflict – the two protagonists with apparently opposite points of view – this matter was raised. I find, very often, that I am thinking as follows:- this is not really my 'best self', this is not my 'spirit mind' but the half-trained, half-educated portion of my mind which has been directed to earth affairs and I want it to know better for another time and so I specifically **instruct** it. This, I realise is a conscious process. I am in fact able to do that and it influences my mind – as distinct from my spirit – henceforward. Would you agree with notions such as that?*

I am wondering how far that process can go. That, I think, is the gist of what I am trying to find out from you.

Abu. Yes indeed. I see that you are referring to the 'Mr. Hyde' and the 'Dr. Jekyll' within yourself. Yes indeed, for I have given you such a picture myself and I have claimed that mankind is showing spiritual advancement – that Dr. Jekyll is slowly overcoming Mr. Hyde, and that is the case, that is as it should be; and that is the process of spiritual evolution and spiritual advancement. It has not proceeded very far upon the earth-plane but your advancement is necessarily or at least potentially, much more rapid when you have quit the earth-plane than whilst you are bounden to it – necessarily so because you will be dwelling in spiritual realms and so many things which may occur to you now, because you live upon a physical, material plane, will no longer do so and therefore the Mr. Hyde will not be goaded into action, as he so frequently is upon the earth-plane, to anything like the same degree. Do you follow?

I would draw a parallel – it is not an analogy, it is closer, it is a parallel – with a person who shall determine to study a certain subject in order that he may become qualified perhaps to function, shall we say as a medical man or as a scientist, upon the earth-plane. He then – or the mind of him – will form the intent so to study and so to apply his mind (and you will please note that here already we have an apparent separation, for his mind is deciding to apply his mind, do you see? There is the same unity in apparent separation which I have endeavoured to explain to you in respect of the spirit mind which we have agreed to call the 'subconscious' and 'conscious' minds, though it is in fact a unity).

This person then, will determine to apply his mind to a course of study in order that he may qualify and advance himself in that particular direction and he will proceed to do so. But a friend, perhaps, will burst in upon him whilst he studies and he will say: "We shall go to the local hostelry and we shall partake of drink. We will go to a place of amusement and we will enjoy ourselves". And the Dr. Jekyll will say:- "But I am desirous of obtaining this advancement and to do so I must attend to my studies". And the Mr. Hyde – who is not necessarily a wicked one, you know – will say:- "Yes, but it would be most pleasant to adjourn to the hostelry". Very well, he will possibly so adjourn – and it may not be of major importance. But if he shall too frequently interrupt his studies for adjournment to the hostelry, the studies will necessarily fall short of what they could have been. And there will be a time limit for there will be the examination which shall determine his status and what he shall have learned and assimilated up to that point will be all that he has available with which he can tackle this examination and so his status will be determined by his own effort, or lack of effort, in that respect. And so with man – as you say.

Consciously and actively – now that your spiritual eyes are open to the circumstances – you, the Dr. Jekyll of you, will be able to review an individual set of circumstances and to come to a conclusion perhaps about them and to make a decision coolly and clearly and, we will trust, rightly – for you have some degree of guidance available to you – and sooner or later shall come the time limit. For whilst you dwell upon the earth there is a time limit – you call it death – and then will be the examination, the *self-examination*. And your spiritual advancement – your status – will have been determined by your Dr. Jekyll – Mr. Hyde conflict, and you will know then the point at which you had arrived, had arrived *at that time*, whilst still living upon the earth-plane, though not fully aware at that time of the circumstances of your advancement.

But upon the examination, which you call death, you *will* become aware. And the process does not cease, for although your environment will be somewhat different, or somewhat differently manipulated and perhaps for a little time somewhat bewildering – (though you will speedily adjust yourselves) – although, as I say, the environment may appear to be somewhat different, the process continues. For you will still have your spirit Dr. Jekyll and your spirit Mr. Hyde, and by the time Mr. Hyde has retired into the background, so that we seldom hear the tread of his rather heavy boot upon the earth-plane (we seldom hear it in Spirit!) you will have made spiritual advancement and you will be dwelling in the region where dwell the Dr. Jekylls. And you shall all be happy together. Will my parallel fit your circumstances and can you make use of it?

As to *how* all this is done – how all this is achieved – I cannot speak as to the mechanics, if any there be, of the process, for it would need that I should touch upon the *nature* of Spirit and I am as unaware of the fundamental nature of Spirit – that is to say of God – as are you yourselves, I think – and I only think – that we, with reasonably logical, thinking minds – human minds – will probably never understand in those terms the nature and the meaning of the Spirit which is God (and which is *you*) simply because the concept transcends mental ability. I do not mean brain ability but the ability of mind itself. It is, as I think – and again I stress the fact that I only think – an emotional matter and emotional matters may not *be* analysed for they are not susceptible of such handling.

51

Questioner. Emotional in the bigger sense of the word?

Abu. In the deep sense of the word, indeed. I am contrasting the intellect with the emotions – the intellectual mind with the emotional body (for there is not an emotional *mind*, there is a contradiction in terms inherent in that phrase) there is not an emotional mind. You may use your intellectual mind to endeavour to dissect the emotions and they will cease to be emotions. There is an 'emotional body' if you care to use the term. I am not suggesting that it is an independent entity, by any means; shall I say then a body of emotion, contained within or rather, inherent in your nature. There is an emotional aspect, an emotional side to you and I *think* – again the stress, I think – that that is the true link with 'God'. The intellect is necessary upon the earth-plane; it has been developed primarily for purposes of earth-dwelling and it has been and is being developed secondarily for processes of induction and deduction, of theorising and postulating, in matters which though possibly transcendental, may yet seem to be less transcendental than might appear, since they *are* susceptible in some degree of intellectual handling. But when you shall dissect your emotion it is no longer an emotion; it is an intellectual concept and ceases to make you feel as once it made you feel, because it is no longer an emotion.

Questioner. Emotion then is the driving thought-force ... or rather the driving force ... thought is not a driving force in the same way.

Second Questioner. Of what nature are the 'distractions from the studies' on your side of life? In what way will Dr. Jekyll be distracted from his studies by Mr. Hyde: what will Mr. Hyde then suggest?

Abu. Very little indeed, my sister. When you shall have reached the stage which I have postulated, where the Dr. Jekylls are in the ascendant – and not till then – you shall settle down happily to your studies, for until you shall have reached that stage (you will recall our 'natural stations') there will necessarily be a degree of conflict and a struggle, for you will become aware of the Mr. Hyde which is part of you and, knowing of the circumstances, you will not be blind. Should there be a proportion of this Mr. or Mrs. Hyde within you, you will endeavour to overcome it. Not to subdue it, but to override and overcome it – it will not be subdued – it will be overlaid and therefore hidden or latent perhaps and because latent quite ready to burst out into force and action again should you invite it so to do. For you do not *destroy* any part of your nature, you merely transcend it, you overlay it; you carry with you the *whole* of your nature – there would be no triumph were it otherwise.

If you shall, by the mere act of dying, become saint-like, then there is no virtue in your rise, for your rise would be purely automatic and not a matter for *you*, but that is not the case. You have a Mr. or Mrs. Hyde; you shall learn of its power and its potency and you shall overcome that power and that potency. You shall find yourself able to say, as mankind is now in some degree able to say:– "I was engendered in the mud; I have risen from that mud and my feet are still planted therein. It is inevitable for I am *engendered* from the mud, but my mind, my head, is in the clouds which are, or can be, Heaven. My feet shall remain in the mud but that is not to say that I shall bedaub my brow with that same mud". That is the position, my sister.

Distractions – yes, happy ones, fortunate ones. For you see, after you have left the earth-plane, there is no longer a time-limit and so you are at liberty as you will to abandon your studies at a moment's notice and to enter with those of your loved ones who shall invite you to do so into pleasant ways, into enjoyments, as you shall wish and you will not be 'wasting time'. That is where the earth-life is unique, in the sense that it is a foreshortened existence and no individual can know how long it may last, and so it were well that the individuals shall make the most of the earth life and not the least. For the more the children shall learn of their dual nature (I do not like the term but you will accept it with me) and the desirability for purely selfish reasons of placing Dr. Jekyll in the ascendant, the easier will that process continue to be when you shall enter into the timeless region where you will have no physical distractions. And distractions which shall have appeal to you may be submitted to for you will not waste time: there is no further examination.

You and you alone, by your efforts alone, will decide the period – the 'time' as it were – of your succeeding transition and there shall be none to goad you and you shall not have to say that "life is fleeting" and we must seize it by the forelock as it passes; that is not the case *after* you have left the earth-plane. And I beg that you will not ask me why this should be, for I do not know.

But I would revert, just for a moment, to some words spoken anent my remarks regarding emotion and intellect, when you spoke of the 'driving thought'.

Questioner. I believe I said "Force".

Abu. In the first instance, but you introduced the word "thought" and you withdrew it and rightly so, for the driving force in the first instance is *interest*. You will say "My interest was aroused" and that has become and does become the driving force which shall impel you to a course of study or an investigation. Your interest was aroused and your interest is an emotion and that emotion will use the intellectual powers of thought in order to satisfy its emotional needs. But whilst the interest is there (in the broad sense of the word an emotional interest as we agreed) the intellect will subserve that emotion and will act as its servant. And when the interest shall depart there will be no longer any occasion for the intellect to apply itself to that particular field of study, whatever it may be. And so you see, the emotional guides and rules the intellectual in such matters, for your interest is an emotion. Your interest is aroused; that is not an intellectual process: the intellectual process follows thereupon.

Chapter Eleven

SUFFERING AND 'ACCIDENTS'

Abu. I will speak a little on a matter which, despite denials, I know is in the minds of more than one of my little audience, that being the matter of suffering – particularly suffering due to illness, sickness, maladjustment of the physical body – which I know gives rise to consideration and to some little difficulty in the mind at times, particularly when the person concerned has learned something of the divine law and the divine love and the divine intention that man should be happy and fulfilled throughout his life (earth-life as well as spirit-life), and yet there is the incidence of disease and of complaints of various sorts, which appear to come unsought and which do not appear to have any valid reason for their existence.

An explanation, I know, is given by certain earth-dwellers, to the effect that such illnesses, such complaints, are the automatic result of an ill-spent life, perhaps a life in a "previous incarnation".

But, I would refute this. In my experience and within my knowledge, this is not the case at all. These accidents – for accidents they are – are accidents in the sense that they are not part of any plan. They are not brought upon you as punishment. They are not even given to you for the better purging or refinement of your spirit.

That is not the case at all. If the individual does find himself, or herself, able to surmount the difficulties and the distress and the occasional bitterness which is brought upon him – his spirit – by physical disabilities – if the spirit is able to surmount these things – then it is all to the good. The spirit has shown fortitude and has certainly taken a step which perhaps it might not have been able to take without the incidence of such complaint. But I will not have it that the complaint was *given* to the individual for such a purpose. It is not part of the plan that man should suffer physically or mentally or spiritually. It is again, as I was discussing with you on a recent occasion, a matter of evolution.

The spirit which forms the aggregation of cells into the physical body – which directs their formation – wishes to work and endeavours to work towards the "nearest of perfection" that can be conceived, and the spirit-conception is, of course, perfect in itself. But the spirit, when dealing with physical matter, must deal with obdurate matter which is subject to impacts of various kinds upon your earth-plane, at various times.

There are forces – electro-magnetical forces – there are forces from the darker side of the spirit world, there are the seemingly accidental happenings both before and after the birth of a child, all of which may and do have an effect upon the cell formation – upon the manner in which the cells are aggregated – and upon the actual cell-formation itself. The spirit, having to the best of its ability built up this body, must thereafter inhabit the body, or *inform* the body (which is a far better word) regardless of disabilities which may exist but which were no *intent* of the spirit in the first place. So, these things, regrettably, at the present stage of your evolution, must be suffered by the spirit. If the spirit can turn them to good purpose, all well and good. If it cannot, it is not of great importance because it is not a *spiritual* matter but a purely physical one.

54

I do not think I need go much further along these lines. It is merely a question of trying to disabuse the minds of any who may hear me of a feeling of "punishment" perhaps, or of a feeling that ill is sent upon mankind by a loving God for His own inscrutable purposes. This is not the case.

Questioner. The spirit that informs the bodies of human beings has, I suppose, to be distinguished in some way, or separated if not distinguished, from, the spirit that must inform matter as such.

I cannot, myself, conceive of matter held together by force, as it must be, unless that force is a "spirit force". There seem to be two orders of spirit, or at least a distinction of some sort which I cannot grasp.

Abu. A distinction, but a distinction with no difference. Spirit is spirit, wherever found, whenever found. Spirit is divine, is of God, is God, and therefore unchanged and unchangeable – invariable. But, it may be portions of this spirit – force may be differentiated, may, as in the case of man, become individualised and self-conscious, yet the spirit, the force which holds together the rocks, which animates the plants, which controls and informs the animal kingdom and which individualises finally upon earth in man himself, is one and the same influx.

It is a question of evolution, but evolution in terms of the differentiation or coalescence of part of the spirit-force. You will recall modern cosmology? You will recall also, then, that empty space, so called, is not in fact empty, but consists of atoms – small particles of gaseous matter, widely separated; and that under certain circumstances a number of these atoms will begin – apparently of themselves – to coalesce and form what I believe are called "nebulae". The nebulae in turn condense still further and form a multitude of stars or suns. And there you have an analogy. For empty space itself contains – almost consists of – the very matter of which the suns consist, but the suns are, as it were, individualised.

Does that help at all in the matter of spirit-power? It is the same thing – exactly the same thing – and the one comes, as it were, from the other: at least it is a parallel process. But there is differentiation, distinction, no *difference*.

Questioner. But, when you use the word "accident" or "accidental", you are referring, I imagine to the action of a spirit-force in a sphere that is non-human, are you not?

Abu. When I speak of accident I refer to both human and non-human. For example, it is "accidental" as far as the great scheme of things is concerned that you should have volcanoes which burst into eruption occasionally, for no true purpose is served by such outbursts and they are not within the plan of the formation of a "ball" – a sphere – upon which spirit can individualise and can incarnate and can become man. Correspondingly you have the diseases and complaints of the physical body of man, which are largely accidental in the same sense.

Questioner. The difficulty, I believe, is this. We have conceived of an all-powerful divine power which would appear to be responsible for whatever happens – whether a volcanic eruption or whatever it may be, because that eruption is the manifestation of a force and a force proceeds from some source. Now, the only ultimate source of all force can be, it seems to us, the one divine source or power.

Abu. You are right. Responsible for – "responsible" is the operative word. Certainly the divine force, which is the force of spirit, is responsible for all that occurs, but it is not necessarily with *intent* that certain of these things shall occur.

It must be borne in mind that the divine intent deals with the *spirit* of man and only, quite secondarily, with the physical body and even then only in so far as the physical body has repercussions upon the spirit.

Hence I permit myself to speak of accident, not in the sense of a "miraculous" happening – something which is beyond the control of and outside the *knowledge* of the all-informing spirit – but something which is beyond and outside of the *intent* of the informing spirit, since it has no great spiritual importance.

Here again of course, arises the difficulty of my own relative remoteness from your sphere of operations. It is so difficult – it must be so difficult – for earth-dwellers to be resigned to or even to accept, such happenings as wars and earthquakes and tidal waves, which cause great destruction and apparent loss of life – it must be very difficult indeed. For us, as in the previous case, no problem exists because we see primarily and almost wholly the *spiritual* side of these happenings.

Hence, I permit myself to use the word "accident"; but in the sense only, as I must insist, that these things are not intentionally and wittingly given to you – brought upon you – for some inscrutable purpose. That is not the case.

In that sense they are truely "accidental", but, in the wider sense, in the broader outlook, they are comprised in the general scheme of things because, as you rightly observe, they are due to force and the force is energised by spirit power acting under the laws which have been laid down and which will not be abrogated.

You, as earth-dwellers, have quite a "glimpse" into the physical laws which control your universe. Certain of you are getting an appreciation of what you are learning to know as "psychic" laws which bring into relation with yourselves the next sphere of existence.

But to go further than that would, as you suggest, be impossible for your finite, limited minds.

I do not extol myself. *My* mind is also finite and limited, but my limitations are perhaps a little further away. I do not claim to know the divine laws in full, naturally. That is impossible until one shall reach infinity, towards which we can but strain our eyes at present.

In many cases the spirit world – perhaps I myself and certainly the dwellers upon planes closer to your earth – can and do "put a finger into the pie" – subject always to the laws. We cannot, even if we would, abrogate them in any way at all but we are permitted upon occasion – more than permitted, we are *required* when called upon for help, for assistance – to direct – perhaps to urge, only gently perhaps, but none the less to urge – the spirit, the mind, of man to give its attention in a certain direction rather than in another direction, and thus we can, to a very small degree, "manipulate" the course of events. Just here and there it is

56

even possible for spirit-power actually to manipulate physical objects, as is seen in your séance rooms when the "children play with the toys".

Since, as I have told you, we can work almost solely through the mind of men, the "reactions", as you call them, of that mind will have and must have a great bearing upon our success or non-success in regard to influencing such minds, most certainly. And there of course comes in the question of environment and heredity and preconceived ideas and the closed mind, and that is why very largely we find ourselves able to work with extreme facility upon one person and with the utmost difficulty, or not at all, upon another. The one upon whom we cannot work, whom in fact we cannot *aid*, is confirmed in his opinion, either that we do not exist at all – that there is no God or that the God is a vengeful God – or something of such a nature, because we are quite unable to do anything with a mind in such a condition. But there are others, more fortunate perhaps, (personally I would say more "educated" more "evolved") through whom we *can* work, and they can be aided, can be assisted, to a much greater degree. And, furthermore, even if the material situation under which they suffer cannot be ameliorated considerably, then at least the individual can be given a degree of peace and mental comfort which otherwise he could not attain alone.

You will understand that the situation as between the spirit-people and those who dwell upon your earth-plane is not a simple, clean-cut issue. We cannot manipulate your world, as occasionally you wish that we could: it just cannot be done. We can only bring influences to bear, and the responsiveness or otherwise of the human-kind upon whom we bring these influences to bear has a considerable effect upon the result – or lack of result. Even a mental condition – a condition of sadness, of grief, of bitterness – even that sort of thing, can and does have a considerable effect upon our ability to enter into the mind of any individual.

Never, I can assure you – never – is there any lack of *desire* to help and to aid you to the utmost of our capacity.

What we do not do is not done because we cannot do it – not because we would not. And there you have, in a small manner, what I have already given to you as the conception of the love of God. The loving God has no *intention* whatever that you shall suffer. It is His intention that you shall be happy. There are laws which He will not change because, were He to change them, He would change Himself and He is unchangeable. There are laws which will not be changed and under which you must live. And we also must live under laws – a slightly modified set of laws, perhaps. But, if those laws work to the hurt of an individual, it is not the intent of the loving God that that individual should suffer such hurt, and it becomes an "accidental" circumstance, in the terms that I have indicated.

Chapter Twelve

THE GIFT OF MEDIUMSHIP

Questioner. The more I see into the relationship between earth and spirit existence the more value I am disposed to place upon what we call 'mediumship'. For most people the spoken word and the experience of spirit personality is a far more potent influence than the inspirational teaching or guidance obtained by what is often called 'direct' contact.

If this be so, 'mediumship' must be a very precious gift, carrying with it a special responsibility, so that what we need is more and more 'faithful instruments'! Will this eventually be recognised, do you think?

Abu. A question fraught with possibilities in the answering for I find myself compelled to say that 'much depends'. Yes, I am with you that 'mediumship', in the terms of your question, is a precious gift, for it is the *only* link between the world of spirit and the world of spirit incarnate, or imprisoned in the flesh. And it is so arranged – it was so arranged. And I have told you that in the long ages past the linkage was much more close and more near and more real and personal than is usually the case today. Largely because the intellect of man has overlaid what you would undoubtedly call the psychic faculties, and there was grave danger of those psychic faculties being stamped virtually out of existence altogether by various means into which I will not go fully at the moment.

It was firstly by the attack upon the mediums and secondly by the materialistic approach which, as I have already said, was necessary in order to destroy a great deal of superstition. The two combined together represented a grave threat to the only link which exists between the two modes of existence. Therefore, mediumship as it exists today, is undoubtedly a precious gift since it is relatively rare.

But, you must not differentiate, for in my eyes there is no differentiation. So I ask that you do not try to differentiate, between what you have called inspiration and what you have called perhaps a more immediate approach, by the use of a physical body, by the use of an implement – a board or a hand for writing, for any of various purposes.

All is mediumship in that the individual concerned is the 'medium' for passing information (and occasionally blessing) through from the wider realm to the more narrow one.

And so all mediumship stands upon the same footing: there is not a 'high' form of mediumship and a 'low' form of mediumship – it is a matter of application. And the lowest possible form of mediumship, if one shall conceive of such, which is applied in the direction of the law of love, is in fact higher than the highest possible achievement of the same thing which is directed to less worthy ends.

And so I ask that you will not try to differentiate: for mediumship, in my eyes, stands upon the one footing; it is the link – more or less satisfactory; yes, by all means in some cases very satisfactory, very pleasingly so – in others quite the reverse, but none the less a *link* – a tenuous thread if you will, but none the less a link and therefore precious.

That being the case, your question goes on to ask – would it not be well to develop a greater number of mediums?

Questioner. My actual words – carefully chosen – were 'faithful instruments'.

Abu. To touch upon that point as a side issue, with regard to your words 'faithful instruments' I must point out that we, in the spirit world, who wish to make communication with you upon the earth can but use what is available.

If a person shall be gifted with the psychic make-up which permits of communication, the faithfulness or otherwise of the instrument does not come into the question. We must use what we find.

Questioner. I think my words were misleading. I meant 'faithful' in the sense of what we call 'fidelity' in one of our wireless instruments – reproducing without distortion.

Abu. That is a question of what I must call quality of reproduction. You speak of your wireless instrument as a faithful instrument for reproduction but is it not the case that in its earlier days it was far less faithful than it now is yet it was none the less valuable? And so the faithfulness – that is to say the certainty of reproducing in your world of matter the ideas which are transmitted from our world of spirit – is a question for development and evolution and it is not possible for *us* to raise the level of faithful reproduction in any given instrument. We must work through what we are offered – or refrain from working, do you see that?

That, I think, will answer that aspect of the question. But, in more general terms, yes indeed, it is our one cry. Give us more instruments – poor ones if you will, but instruments through whom foolish, childish things can be done – yes, it matters not so that there is a conviction brought to the viewer or the listener that an extra-mundane power is at work – something that will give the onlooker cause to think.

Instruments of a high mental capacity? Whether it be of a high spiritual order or not is not very material from our point of view. It is, from the point of view of the individual but, from our point of view it does not matter much. If there is a high mental standard then that instrument can be used for the propagation of more of the ideas of spirit than could be the case through a less erudite medium. The spirituality of the medium does not come into that question – not at all – and so I am with you, heart and soul, give us more instruments. The better they are the better we shall be pleased, but, instruments, please, at all costs.

You are, as it is right that you should be, a seeker after perfection; you desire perfection as we all would desire perfection but you would not be so foolish as to refuse the mediocre because the perfect is not yet available. And so, we will make do with the mediocre, so that we can have a word with our children upon earth from time to time. And we look forward, in God's good time, to the perfection of this link, for it will develop, it will extend, it will grow – it cannot be otherwise.

And so we are of good cheer, of good heart. It may be a slow process in your eyes and in mine. It is certainly a painful process, for, with me I know, you would wish to expedite the thing, you would wish to take the whole of mankind and shake them until they could see what is under their nose – but they will not. They cannot do it – we can but follow the channels.

I cannot say that I would give a specific and particular blessing to mediums, to instruments, because, though that is not an accidental matter, it is a matter beyond *your* organising and beyond mine. It is, shall I say, a God-given gift and therefore I cannot give special commendation to a medium just because the person is a medium, but I can and do commend the medium who puts that gift into service. For there are many, there are many indeed, who, because of worldly position, because of one thing and another, because of fear of contumely or vituperation or something of the kind, whilst being fully aware that they are able to do, to see and to hear things which normal people do not hear and do not see, will keep quiet about it. I cannot give a blessing there, but, where one shall find that there is a little grasp of the contact with the next world and appreciation of its value, and that one shall put that gift to service, no more can be asked. I am happy indeed to commend such a one.

Chapter Thirteen

INHIBITING FACTORS IN COMMUNICATION

Questioner. Is there some inhibiting factor involved in the very fact of communication, so that complete communion would defeat its own ends? And why does it seem to be the case that the phenomena of mediumship are less striking today than they were?

Abu. If your question shall ask me why is it difficult to bring to the children of earth final and incontrovertible evidence of survival, I reply that I do not know. It may be (I have touched upon what was referred to as the Golden Age in the past) it probably is the fact that were communion between the two modes of existence more free, more simple, more easily attained, man would become – as indeed he did then become – dissatisfied with his earthy existence and would not give it the attention that he must give it. Man is incarnate upon the earth, that is a fact – I have referred to it as an 'experiment' – but it is none the less a fact, which is apparent and which must be allowed for; if then man were as nearly and closely in touch with the spirit world as you would wish him to be, he would speedily become too dissatisfied with the limitations and the difficulties of the earth conditions to give that phase of his existence the attention which it must have. That is one possible reason why there are difficulties in communication.

The material reasons, the mechanical reasons, for the difficulties, will probably make themselves apparent to *you*; I need not go into that aspect; for you will find it at least as difficult to get into communication or communion with even a dog as it is for us to get into communication with you, but, given patience, given goodwill on both sides, given all these things (and they include an appreciation of the essential brotherhood between yourself and brother dog) you *can* get into a degree of communion with your dog. Consider, for instance, the training of animals, not always conducted under fear and with cruelty, for many animals would not respond to such as they do. You have a breed of dog, as I believe, which is most intelligent and is used to control a relatively foolish creature such as sheep, and these dogs achieve an understanding of their master's wishes and desires which indicates a communion, a communication, between them which is as powerful and as effective as the communion which we have established with you. I do not draw a parallel you are not in the position of sheep and we of dogs! I refer only to the difficulties of communication. If then mediums or instruments will but offer themselves, will but undergo the necessary – quite necessary and sometimes very lengthy – period of development and training, we will use them, we will certainly use them, do not fear.

You have suggested and I believe it to be the case that the results of mediumship apparent in your midst now are rather less striking than once they were. That I do not think to be the case in so far as teaching is concerned, but the signposts may be fewer, the physical phenomena and manifestations may be fewer and less striking than was the case in the past. Man quite speedily tends to become blasé, and that has much to do with it. For, when a medium or instrument shall appreciate the fact of his sensitivity, his ability perhaps to see, to hear a little, to permit one or more of us to use his organism through which we may

61

speak, he will be wishful to put that into operation, as indeed we wish him to do, but he may speedily become satisfied with what is happening through his instrumentality and may feel reluctant to spend a further period of, it may be, years, in refraining from public demonstrations of his gift – albeit the gift is of value – in order that the said gift may be builded up yet more strongly. I do not say that this is always the case and I do not condemn such cases as exist – it is but natural – but it has bearing upon the point.

I will give you very hastily parallel cases. For example, in the early days of Christianity – right or wrong, well-guided or misguided, is beside the point – there were those who were nothing short of fanatical. They had enthusiasm, vast enthusiasm; they were burned, they were tortured, they were crucified; but still they builded up this concept with fanaticism and with enthusiasm. One does not see quite so much of this enthusiasm today; men have become blasé in that respect – this apart from the fact that the philosophy to which I refer has become overlaid with much that is worthless and even harmful; (I do not discuss that point at this stage). You have seen the same thing in various religious sects, that an enthusiasm will arise, there will arise giants of oratory, giants even in cases of healing, giants even of apparent miracle-working, and then the thing becomes accepted. Man is a sophisticated creature, he becomes blasé, and unless he shall be constantly dazzled with something yet greater, something yet newer, something yet more striking, he tends to settle down to a quiet, rather dead level in which there is little enthusiasm. And that is part of the explanation of the fact that the quality and quantity of mediumship appear to have declined to some extent.

But it will not always be so; we have set our hands to this plough anew, we have found the soil fertile and it is goodly soil. It is difficult, it is recalcitrant at times – it could not be otherwise – for what has had to be done has necessarily resulted in many stones in the way, in a hardness of heart and of mind, because man for so long has been misled and much has had to be broken down and cast aside. But the soil is goodly soil and in it shall grow the fruit, the crop, the flowers that we are anxious to generate upon earth. We have set our hands, as I say, to this plough: the time for harvest is not yet – a little later – but we shall not allow the message, the one message, the only message, to be stultified, to fade away, to die for want of phenomena, of 'manifestations'. You will have your phenomena again; I would remind you that the giants who were mediums in days gone by have not very long left your earthplane; it is but a short time, they are all but contemporary, and therefore the records can be substantiated, can be looked up, which is not the case with other expressions of religious thought and philosophy, and we shall not wait until the effect, the result of the labours of the giants, has become quite forgotten and set aside before we shall insist upon and shall produce a recrudescence of such matters as shall again call the attention of man to our existence and therefore to the existence of our Father – which is the important point. My answer is not complete, I am aware of that, but it is a lengthy subject and a difficult one.

As a rider to what I have said I will add just this; I have spoken on earlier occasions about the growing interest which is being taken and will be taken by men of science in these phenomena, hitherto regarded as totally unscientific. You have referred me to the doings of the giants of mediumship of earlier days and I will venture to refer you to the acts which will be forthcoming of the scientific giants in later days to the same end – to the same end – that men shall be brought to know of their continued existence – not a resurrection but a continuance of existence – and of their essential brotherhood, and following therefrom, of the love of our Father. And that is the message: I do not think I can usefully take it any further.

Chapter Fourteen

LANGUAGES AND 'COLOURATION'

Questioner. We have often noticed that you use words in speaking to us which your instrument would not have used. The whole question of 'colouration' and of language is to us very confusing and I cannot put my question in a simple form.

Abu. The question is itself an involved matter and I can sympathise with your difficulty in presenting it simply and concisely and I trust that you will sympathise with me in that I am unable to explain it simply and concisely because of its complex nature. How then am I to answer you understandably?

I will give you a little parallel – of which I am fond – and I will speak to *you*, for as I have been given to understand, you were born and lived in a country other than this and the tongue which you now speak is not your native tongue. There was a time when as an adult person you had occasion to learn the language which you now speak with such fluency, and whilst you were learning you had necessarily to attach certain meanings to certain sounds, for that, put shortly, is the process of learning a language, is it not? And the very business of remembering that what you in your mother tongue had called something completely other was now "a table" was a conscious, witting effort on your part; you had to remember that the word for this thing which you pronounced otherwise was in this new language to be pronounced "table".

Now at that time the conscious mind of you was delving into the storehouse of your own subconscious ability to produce or reproduce through your own vocal mechanism certain sounds which, until you began to learn this new language, would have held no meaning at all for you, but now in learning this language you are given firstly the meaning – the sound that is to say which has had a meaning for you in your own tongue and which refers for example to a table – and you have had to learn that when referring to this article of furniture you must now say "table", thereby consciously making use of your ability to produce or reproduce sound, that ability being already in existence within your subconsciousness but being applied in a new fashion by your conscious mind. Do you follow me so far?

Then the position is somewhat parallel with regard to the communication which I am now making to you, for it was the spirit mind of you which prompted and originated your learning of the new language. You will recall our little talk upon the matter of *learning* and in what learning consists – the seizing upon and adopting by the subconscious mind of those ideas or sounds which shall be implanted within it, the making of those things its own, so that they are immediately available (except when memory shall be at fault) for the use of the conscious mind. And a similar process occurs here and now, for when, upon learning this new language, you shall wish to refer to a table, the *idea* of a table was the first step in your mind and that was not clothed in any words at all. Up to a point you had been clothing it in certain sounds which would have conveyed the idea of a table to one of your compatriots; now you have learned to refer to it by means of other sounds – "table" to wit – sounds which are recognised by those whose tongue is this which you now speak. They recognise in the pronunciation of the syllables the idea which was in the first instance within the spirit mind of you – not the subconscious, the underlying spirit mind – which was anxious to set forth an idea; but that idea to be communicated must be clothed in words, and I am in the same position.

I wish to come among my children and in order that I may seize the first opportunity of inserting my artful little message: I am desirous of coming among you and informing you again and again that God is Love, and if I shall merely send forth that thought *as a thought* from my own spirit mind, it will in all probability reach *your* spirit minds, but in equal probability it is doubtful whether your conscious minds would even become aware of the fact, for – in parenthesis – I have told you often that for you a great deal goes on in a realm where the greater part of your mind dwells of which you will never become aware whilst you are limited by the flesh, because of the inhibiting nature of the fleshly vessel. Very well then, I express – telepathically is I believe the word – the idea that God is love and, if you shall receive it within your spirit minds, as you probably will, you will respond to the thought which I have passed to you and *I* shall appreciate your response but you may not even appreciate having received the message, still less that you have responded to it, for your conscious mind will not even be aware of the circumstances.

If then I am to make a communication to you, I must, for it to be effective, send it to you in a form which is graspable and assimilable by your conscious minds, and it can then be transferred to the great storehouse of your *sub*conscious mind where the subconscious, conjoined with the spirit itself (I used the term 'spirit-mind' but I would wish to withdraw 'mind' and refer only to the spirit: I do not, as you know, wish to confuse you with too many 'minds') your subconscious mind then will assimilate this information handed to it by the conscious mind, which has seized upon the information given to you by myself, and the spirit will con over what is being newly given to the subconscious mind and will relate it to what the spirit itself is telepathically – or instinctively, if you will – aware of as being – in its own terms – well-founded, and the subconscious mind will thereupon, at the dictate of the spirit of course, pigeonhole this piece of information for subsequent use when the conscious mind shall reach in, in order to produce it and bring it forth in words. I am becoming very involved indeed; I can but trust that you are following. The argument, though involved, is, you will find, quite logical.

Very well then, I have what we have agreed to call a subconscious mind which is available for the use of my spirit. I do not *need* a conscious mind because I can transfer any portion of the informations which exist within my subconscious mind to any other subconscious mind dwelling in spirit and not confined and limited by the flesh, without any effort, and therefore I do not need a conscious mind, neither do I need a language. But, if I am to communicate with my children here upon earth, I must perforce make use of language and it is a laborious business, as you will appreciate. It is a laborious business for a baby to learn to speak at all and to convey its thought by this so roundabout and inefficient method, and it is laborious for me to learn to perform this particular function and to exercise it having learned it.

I have then a subconscious mind: the instrument whom I am at present using has of course also a subconscious mind and I can transfer some of the content

(content of ideas, you understand) from my subconscious mind directly to his subconscious mind because it *is* a subconscious mind, though his *conscious* mind in a waking state might not and probably would not be aware of that. It might possibly reject the information, unless it shall be presented in an acceptable form, because it did not originate it and therefore the information arriving at the conscious side of the mind is a little suspect, since it comes in or appears to come in by the 'back door' as it were. I then transfer ideas, notions, into the subconscious mind of my medium and if I shall not find therein any strong objection to what I am proposing to put forth among you, the mechanism by which the ideas which I am now injecting into the subconscious mind are converted into audible words acts in the main as an automatic one. You see, my instrument has learned to talk and therefore I do not have to make the 'machine' talk: all I have to do is, as it were, to press the same automatic button which the spirit of my medium has learned to press and *his* instrument – his physical body – will respond for me as it responds for him.

Questioner. Given that process in action, as you have described it, could it be that, if the conscious mind offered resistance of some sort, there might be some difficulty in expressing certain ideas?

Abu. Either difficulty in expressing the ideas or colouration of the message. Yes, with this proviso: you have referred to an objection within the conscious mind, a difference of opinion, a disagreement – but within the *conscious* mind of the medium, you will recall. Now, is it conceivable to you – I trust that it is for it is the fact – that there may be disagreement between the medium's conscious views and his subconscious views, for that is the case; and my medium is not unique, it is the case with all mankind. Then, should I wish to express views which run contrary to views already consciously expressed by the medium when in a state of wakefulness, it is conceivable that I shall find no objection – because none such exists – in his subconscious area. When he shall hear my words subsequently (through your 'wonderbox' perhaps) his conscious mind, the conscious *side* of his mind, may quite justly, reasonably and logically say: "But, *I* do not think thus". And indeed his conscious mind does not think thus, but his subconscious is greater than his conscious and his conscious mind cannot be aware of all that passes in his subconscious. And so there may be objection and disagreement on a narrow issue such as that, whilst we are in fact in reasonable agreement upon the broad issue.

But you have rightly suggested that if there shall be a fundamental, a basic, disagreement within the subconscious mind of my medium then I would either have great difficulty in passing my message through at all or alternatively, if I were to *insist* upon forcing it through, it would almost certainly be coloured.

Questioner. The subconscious mind can be impressed and taught by the conscious mind, but if the conscious mind holds some view very strongly and you try to put through a completely different view, do I gather that the subconscious mind will not accept it and let it pass?

Abu. It will *endeavour* to reject it. You have said that the subconscious mind is

66

impressed and informed by the conscious and that is perfectly true, but you will not forget my earlier remarks to the effect that I can 'sneak in' by the back door to a degree, for I also am subconscious, as is the mind of the medium, and his conscious mind is unaware of the impressing unless and until it shall filter through.

Questioner. One further question on the 'colouration' business. In the opposite case, where so far from holding any objections, the conscious mind is deeply interested in the matter and nurses some special convictions about it, might it accept it and add some colouration of its own?

Abu. You have used the word 'colouration' and the colouration may be either positive or negative. The message – the portion of the message which I am endeavouring to pass through – may be, in circumstances such as you describe, a little 'highly coloured' perhaps; that is conceivable and indeed it does occur.

Questioner. In such a case, would you yourself be fully aware that such colouration was taking place?

Abu. No my child, regretfully and regrettably, I am not able to be fully aware. I receive your response and I gain some indication of course from your response as to whether I have pressed the right button and pressed it correctly and have succeeded in impinging upon you with the type and kind of information that I am wishful to impart. But I would make this small point, that I am linked very closely indeed with this present instrument. I have been, may I say, 'developing' him for this purpose for a long time – for a long time before I came within your ken, my son – and there was a purpose, there was an end in view, and I am therefore in very close touch indeed, and I would imagine – more particularly from what I have heard from you and through the 'wonderbox' as also from the information which I can tap from the mind of my medium himself – I would imagine, I say, that my message comes through to you in as close an approach to its pristine origin as can be expected. Some colouration is unavoidable but, if I may differentiate, there is no distortion.

This medium, is a subject of "Libra". I have spoken upon the subject of Astrology: do not then berate me for using such a term; I make use of it with no occult significance beyond that which you will find I have already expressed in my talk. This subject, then is Libra. It is a sign which indicates a balance (in so far as a balance can be achieved) a necessity for probing and investigating and of listening to both sides of a question, if there shall be two sides, and of endeavouring to weigh them, making such judgment as is possible according to the state of the mind on that particular subject, and of accepting that which is to him – the medium – reasonable and of rejecting that which is to him unreasonable. Now, I may put through, or may endeavour to put through, a proposition which to him might be unreasonable and I would succeed in getting such a proposition through because I should be using the subconscious mind of my medium to which the 'unreasonable' proposition is not so unreasonable after all, do you see?

That is why I wished for an instrument of this calibre, with a reasonable adequacy of vocabulary – not for my own enhancement, not for my own advancement, but because I am aware, as you are aware, and I *was* aware, as you were *not* aware, of the nature and the type of the children to whom I should be speaking and of the vital necessity therefore for an adequacy of expression, do you see? I am drawing the 'veil' a little aside for you but you will appreciate that not only on my part but on the part of many others a great deal of preparation has been done for such a simple matter as this. And were it not that our message is, as is admitted, a vital one for the spirit of man incarnate upon the earth – were it not so – the effort on both sides, which is necessary in order that this message should be propagated – that effort would not be worth while.

For it is indeed an effort, I assure you, in all directions, but our message *is* vital. Men have died – perhaps by the thousand – in order to endeavour to propagate this message, according to their lights. Men have suffered ignominy; there have been all the troubles to which earth is subject because of this vital message which may not be suppressed or overlaid or even *transcended*. It is a simple message and it must not be transcended by complication which shall lose its virtue. And so we – the spirit world – who have always endeavoured to keep in touch of course, as you will be aware, have made great efforts of recent decades in your earth time in order that the message should once again be brought before mankind in a simple form, in an assimilable form, in an acceptable form – supported, as it has been, by evidence which shall satisfy and convince man that these persons who bring to him such a message have the right to do so, for they *know* that of which they are speaking. And so the effort was made, the effort is still being made, and the message is being spread.

Chapter Fifteen

LANGUAGES AND THE SUBCONSCIOUS MIND

Questioner. You have explained that it was not necessary, in your particular state of advancement, to 'learn a language', since you can, by some method unknown to us, use the subconscious mind of your instrument. Supposing that you had not had an instrument of good intelligence, with a particularly large vocabulary, would you have found it as easy to have spoken to us with the ready flow of language that you command, or could it have been done in some other way?

Abu. My answer to your question must be twofold. You have stated that it is not necessary for me to 'learn' the English language and that is true, but in order that I may make use of this instrument as I now do it has been necessary for me to learn how to do *that* – how to make use of the instrument – but that has not required the learning of a language in the same manner as you upon earth must learn a foreign language.

The fact of the ability to control and make use of the subconscious mind and the content of the subconscious mind of an instrument is a matter for learning, a matter for appreciation (I cannot find the precise word to describe the process for you have none) and I have learned to do that, so that, as I have already explained to you, I could, were it desirable, take control of an instrument of another nationality and make use of the storehouse within *his* subconscious and that would include the use of *his* native language. But that is not to say that I as an individual would therefore be able to *speak* that language, for it is not so.

It is a process rather of conversion, just as the greater mind of this my instrument, when in possession of his conscious senses, converts his own wordless thought into words by a process as mysterious to me as it must be to you. I do not know the mechanism and it is not necessary that I should know the mechanism because in making use of a body such as this I do not any longer have to use such mechanism, but in making use of this subconscious content I have available what *he*, my instrument, has available, and the process is the same.

You have referred to the vocabulary: since this my instrument has a reasonably efficient vocabulary, I find generally speaking a sufficiency of words to serve my purpose and I feel reasonably sure that since my application to the matter in hand is greater than his is normally required to be, it is probable that I, whilst making use of his body, do in fact make use of a greater vocabulary than he is accustomed to doing; but the vocabulary is still his and is still available to him, if he shall apply himself as I apply myself to his subconscious mind.

Questioner. But would you not find it more difficult if you were using a medium who had not such a vocabulary?

Abu. I will come to that point immediately. There is a slight contradiction in the first place, for if I who am wishful to bring to the children teachings which I suppose may be described as philosophical, should be offered the use of an

69

entirely unsuitable instrument, I would regretfully decline the honour for there would be no point in my endeavouring to make use of such an instrument for it would not serve my purpose. I would find myself so handicapped by the lack of content of the subconscious mind that I would be quite unable to get my message to you and there would be no point in my endeavouring so to do unless I should be content to take the lengthy and laborious process of educating the subconscious mind of the medium in question without at the same time educating his conscious mind, and that is, as I have said, necessarily a lengthy and laborious process; but it can be done and in certain instances, where it has been deemed desirable, it has been done.

I have already expressed myself as being fortunate in that I have found an instrument which I can use with reasonable facility, whose subconscious mind is a reasonably adequate storehouse (it is not sufficient) to be of use to you and that I have gathered about me a body of children whose minds are receptive to the teachings and at the same time are keen and will seize upon points which I shall make and will discuss them intelligently. And so the trinity which is necessary is as complete and as perfect, I think, as could be hoped; it is very far from perfect, you will appreciate that, but it is as perfect as can be hoped.

I myself the teacher, with the ideas, with the thoughts, with the philosophies within my own mind, clearly known, clearly held, and I am able to express them clearly in my own sphere. The instrument, a reasonably efficient channel. The ears which take heed to my message, receptive and intelligent in their reception. More than that we cannot ask; the conditions, the situation, the circumstances, could ideally be considerably improved and I have promised quite faithfully that upon the, to me happy occasion when you, my children, shall join me in *these* spheres, we will indeed hold 'discussion groups' such as you cannot hold upon earth, for your own eyes will be more widely opened and your own minds will necessarily be more receptive and I shall be more in my element and shall be able to speak more freely and more easily than is possible at present. That is the position.

Questioner. We know that you were not English and English was not your native language, but would it be possible for you to speak through any instrument in your own language? Is it necessary for the instrument to know the language?

Abu. No, my child, it is not necessary for the instrument to know the language but it is necessary for the communicator, myself to wit in the case which you put forward, to place within the subconscious knowledge of the instrument – *sub-conscious* knowledge you will remark – the ability to pronounce the words of the language which it is desired to put forth; whether that language shall have meaning for the instrument or not does not matter. The probability is that it will not have meaning, it will be a mere jumble of sounds, and since I am well able to convey, though a little imperfectly as I have explained to you, the ideas which I wish to lay before you by using the natural language of the instrument, again there seems to me little point in undergoing a laborious process of translating as it were from the English which is natural to this subconscious mind into a language such as that which you would call ancient Egyptian, which is totally unnatural and foreign and which would have no meaning whatever for either the instrument or for you, my children.

Questioner. If we suppose some person – a not very advanced spirit – and shall we say of French nationality, who has but recently passed over, yet is able to control this medium, he would not be able speak to us in any other language than French, I imagine, since that is the only language he knows, and he is not in so advanced a state as to be able to use the subconscious mind of the instrument. Is that so?

Abu. That is largely true except that, in a case such as that which you postulate, it is almost certain that the subconscious mind of the medium – itself active during this process – might and probably would, intersperse words of English with the French natural to the communicator, for, as has been explained to you, it is impossible that any communication shall come to the earth-plane through a medium, as necessarily it must come, perfect and uncontaminated by its passage through the subconscious mind of the medium who is being used. That subconscious mind must come into question and the only matter which arises is how *much* of that subconscious mind necessarily comes into the question, and that I cannot determine and you perhaps with difficulty can determine, but that is a difficulty which cannot be overcome.

Questioner. So that in the case of a spirit recently come to your side of life – say our Frenchman – he would not be able to communicate with us in English without actually **learning** *that language?*

Abu. He would not be able to use your particular method, he would have to learn the language, because he has, throughout his earthly life, been in the habit of clothing his thoughts in words and in words of a specific language namely in this instance French, and upon passing, and for some time after, he will continue to clothe his thoughts in words and they will be French words, and when he shall make a communication (assuming that he is making it directly as I myself am now communicating and not through the interposition of a guide, which is at least as usual) then he will endeavour to clothe his thoughts in French words. And if he finds the French words within the compass of the subconscious mind which he is using, then he will express himself through the medium in French. But, as I have said, there will probably be English words, English phrases, English idioms perhaps, interspersed with the French, which may even give rise to suspicion upon occasion. That has occurred as I am aware and there of course is the difficulty.

Questioner. Of course proof of survival is given in cases where it is known that the medium has no knowledge of a particular language and yet the spirit has spoken through that medium correctly in that particular language and has been understood by someone among his hearers.

Abu. Yes, that undoubtedly is so, but you are touching upon a very large subject to which there are very many ramifications, for there is firstly the subconscious mind of the medium which is under consideration and there is the conscious, witting, willing mind of the communicator; and if the second – the communicator – shall be a more forceful, a more powerful personality, than the medium then it is more than probable that the communicator will succeed in impressing upon the subconscious of the medium the ability to *pronounce* words which are not within the compass of that subconscious as being *meaningful* (I hope you take my point) – it is a question of balance. If the medium shall him or her self be of a strong and powerful personality it is less likely that his subconscious mind can be so overshadowed as to be able to produce the words of a foreign language unknown to him. It is involved: I fear it is involved.

Questioner. It seems that a peculiarly balanced type of mind would make the best medium – a mind which was receptive in certain ways and yet not merely 'weak'.

Abu. Ready and able to give at the right moment. If you will permit me I will take you all the way to the very end of the road in this direction and I will remind you that each and every one of you – the spirit of you – is using a subconscious mind which is empty of content other than that which *you* have placed within it. If I or some other shall wish to make use of your astral or etheric body, complete with subconscious mind, to operate the physical, we shall then find not only a storehouse which – being able thereto – we can use but we shall find also stumbling blocks which *you* have built in this same storehouse and over which we must trip upon occasion, for it is your storehouse and not ours, do you see?

Questioner. There is one point on which we could usefully put questions – the ability or abilities of the subconscious mind. You spoke for instance of its ability to reproduce what is to all intents and purposes a sound – not a word – a sound without meaning. I imagine that the subconscious mind has many abilities at present very obscure to us and I should be hard put to it to define what it can or cannot do.

Abu. You touch upon a large subject. I am smiling a little because you have differentiated between a sound which has meaning and a sound which has not meaning, for of course it is you who apply the meaning to the sound – the sound as such has no meaning. And there we touch upon the whole question of the multiplicity of languages in use upon the earth-plane. For one individual will see an animal, or perhaps even merely call up a mental picture of an animal and that picture will say "cow", but to his neighbour that picture says "vache"; the words are utterly different but the idea underlying them is identical.

But I broke in upon your question, for part of the question which you put to me referred to the capabilities of the subconscious mind and you imagined that perhaps they were vaster than you can at present understand or conceive and I said that you were touching upon a vaster subject than you appreciated. For, do you see, the mind, the conscious and the subconscious minds, have of themselves no life, no existence, they are merely tools, instruments, for the use of the spirit of you and the subject if pressed further in that direction tends to become unduly mystical perhaps and impossible of grasping and so you are right to confine your attention to mind as such. But you must bear within your mind that that is not the end of the story, for just as the physical body is but an instrument for the etheric and for the mind, so correspondingly the mind itself is but an instrument for the greater spirit. The spirit has no *knowledge* as has the mind, for it does not *need* knowledge, but it has experience. The mind on the other hand has knowledge, for it needs knowledge, but it has no action. The physical body has no knowledge, it is *informed* by the mind, but it has action. And that is how the affair is split up.

Chapter Sixteen

THE CONSCIOUS AND SUBCONSCIOUS MINDS

Questioner. You have told us that when you speak to us in this way, you employ some kind of storehouse of words and ideas normally belonging to your instrument. As we understand that his spirit can at such times function on another plane, with what does he function, since it would seem that all his 'knowledge', so to speak, remains with his astral body at your disposal?

Abu. You are well equipped to answer that question yourselves. I will be a little unkind and I will require that you shall answer it for yourselves.

There is our analogy of a balloon floating upon the water, you will recall. Below the surface is the small arc which contains or consists of what we have agreed to call the conscious mind, and above the surface is the greater reservoir which we have agreed to call the subconscious mind, the spirit mind, that is to say. Now, with which of these two 'compartments' (the compartment that is to say, of the spirit mind belonging to this child of mine whom I am at present using) which of these compartments do you think I need to have recourse to in order to do that which I am now doing – the greater or the lesser? The lesser, the conscious mind, of course. There is the 'descent'.

I have no conscious mind in the sense that you and this my child have a conscious mind, because I am not delimited by earth conditions, but in order to communicate with my children who *are* so delimited I must adopt a conscious mind and so I enter into the person of this my child and there I find available all that which I shall need, (or a great deal that I need – not all), and I leave untouched the superior content of his subconscious or greater spirit mind, which has no reference at all to earth dwelling. That is what he is now functioning with because he is upon spirit and is not functioning upon the earth system at all. And that is the prime reason why it is so rare for a medium in deep trance to bring back any memory as it is called of where he has been and what he has done, simply because the earth-content of the mind is in use in other hands – as in this instance. So you see, you were in a position to answer your own question.

Questioner. I thought the conscious and subconscious 'minds' were really one and that we used some of each when we were functioning here.

Abu. My sister has simplified the picture a little unduly but it is as well that it should remain so for the position is largely as if that were the case, that I, Abu, having no *conscious* mind but having a 'subconscious' mind (from your point of view of course: for me it is just my mind – it is myself) and requiring a conscious mind through which to communicate with my children, borrow one and I borrow the physical organism of this my child in order that I may so communicate. And within the reach of the conscious mind which I am borrowing I am able to tap the contents of the *sub*conscious mind belonging to my medium as well as those existing within my own subconscious mind. But the aspect of the subconscious mind of the medium which is turned 'heavenward' as it were – spiritward, that is to say – and has no reference to earth, remains his for I do not need that part; I have my own and so he – his spirit – is functioning at this present moment, using only *that* part of the mind – the total mind – which is his.

Chapter Seventeen

THE "DEATH" OF THE SOUL-BODY

Questioner. The earth body normally functions for perhaps seventy or eighty years; is there a similar limit set to the functioning of the soul-body or does it depend upon the evolution or progress of each individual spirit? In other words, does the spirit which progresses quickly find it possible to dispense with the soul-body much sooner than would a 'lazy' spirit – if the expression be permissible?

Abu. No, there is no arbitrary time limit at all. The spirit, as of course by this time you are well aware, is eternal and is everlasting and is immutable. It does not change; it is the God-spirit, for it is of the essence. The bodies – the vehicles of manifestation would be a better word but a clumsy one and so I permit myself to use the word 'body' and you will understand that when I say body I do not necessarily mean a flesh and blood body but a vehicle of manifestation – there are many, many such, some of which are created by the spirit for itself, for its use when the spirit is dwelling in more 'rarefied' atmospheres, may I say, but the earlier ones are created by the spirit for a specific purpose in order that the spirit may manifest upon a plane of a certain 'density' such as the earth-plane for example, which requires a physical body for the purpose of manifestation at all. I am with difficulty endeavouring to give you a picture of a spirit – it is so difficult – having, owning, possessing, a large number of bodies and yet not possessing them all at one and the same moment. But with regard to what we have agreed to call the soul-body, the etheric-body, the spirit-body, and its relationship with the physical body, that we have already gone into at length and the spirit-body or the 'soul' is a necessary link between the spirit itself and the physical. That does not necessarily apply further up the scale of 'vibration' and so we will confine ourselves for the moment to dealing with the immediate circumstances as your question suggests.

There is no arbitrary time limit for the simple reason that there is no arbitrary time. It is quite impossible to say that the spirit of man, dwelling in the soul-body on the next plane of existence, will remain there for so and so many years, for there are no 'years'. You can perhaps endeavour to relate the period during which a spirit has been upon the spirit-world – upon the spirit-plane as you would say – to relate that period to the number of your earthly years which have passed by. For example, our mutual friend who tends the door, has, as I understand, been a "spirit", that is to say dwelling in spirit-body only and not in a physical body, for a matter of . . . I do not know . . . forty years, something of that kind (earth years of course) but is that to say that he has undergone forty or fifty earth years' 'worth' of experience upon the spirit-plane? I do not know; I cannot say. You must ask *him*, he will tell you how long in spirit terms he has been there and you will tell him how long in earth terms he has been there.

And so there can be no arbitrary limit. We had a somewhat happy phrase, although a little vague perhaps, which we used some time ago; we spoke of 'psychological time' and the 'psychological moment', and those things, the things of the psyche are of course fundamental, when the psyche is all that you have and you have no physical body with which to clog the psyche.

I am aware that you have already been given suggestions regarding the nature of time which must have been in the highest degree confusing to you and so I will now proceed to confuse that issue still further by remarking that you may envisage two persons who have been what you would call 'dead' for the same length of what you would call "time" – perhaps twenty years, it does not matter – and the one has lived through one hundred years of experience, but they are 'contemporary' in all respects except the psychological aspect. And, since much talk has been held this evening upon the power of thought and, since you will realise that your spirit-body, your very environment, are dependent upon *your* own thought, you will realise that the person who has lived through one hundred years of psychological experience will have amassed a greater 'content' shall I say than the person who has lived through only five years of psychological experience in the same earth time. For the earth time is not a common factor when you come to dwell upon the spirit-plane.

As to the shedding of the etheric, the astral, the soul-body, it is not a gradual process; it could hardly be a gradual process or the unhappy spirit would find itself partly clothed and partly unclothed and would hardly know where it dwelt! It is a matter of leaving, a matter of quitting, as upon the earth-plane you could shed clothing. You would not remain half in and half out of one of your outer garments, it would be uncomfortable, and so you will shed the coat completely or you will wear it completely and if you can envisage your cast-off coat thereupon, in a matter of what you would regard as minutes (it is difficult you see, always this question of time must arise) but if you can envisage your cast-off coat in a matter of minutes evaporating into the atmosphere and being no longer a coat, that is what happens to the etheric-body.

For unless it shall be crystalised, held together, congealed as it were, by the organising force of spirit, it will become undifferentiated once again and it does so quite speedily. It can be held together – here again I am venturesome for I permit myself to touch upon points which will give me trouble in the future, I am well aware – but it is possible, it is just possible for an etheric body – an 'astral shell' is the term, I believe – deliberately to be held together, yet not sentient, intelligent or living, but held together by the power of thought of the spirit who has lately worn it.

Questioner. With what intention?

Abu. With what intent, indeed? I have already said that I was laying up trouble for myself in the future! Would you be so very kind as to make a note of that particular question and hurl it at me upon another occasion? I would not wish to be side-tracked at this moment. With what intention, indeed? If you will do me the favour of thinking over the proposition you will in part answer that question yourselves, I am quite sure.

And now, what points have I left untouched?

Questioner. I don't think you have left any point untouched. I think you have covered the whole of the question because the final part referred to a 'lazy' spirit progressing more slowly . . .

Abu. I have covered that, because you see, your question automatically brings in the question of time; will the one progress *sooner* than the other?

Questioner. I quite understand that one spirit can, in a period of say five years evolve much more rapidly than what I have called a 'lazy' spirit.

Abu. I would not wish that you should use such a word in any sense of disparagement. I do not think that you do and I would wish that you should not, for this reason, that, as I have told you in the past, here there is no compulsion because no compulsion is necessary. The spirit which is not willing and happy to do the things which are consistent with the sphere in which he is dwelling – the sphere of happiness in which he is dwelling – is no longer upon that sphere. There is no compulsion, he does not have either to 'mend his ways' or go; if his ways need mending he is already *not there*. It is a self-contained process. Again, you have the power of thought which does those things quite automatically for you, and by the application of your thought-power you can, when you wish, raise yourself to the level to which you are suited (but not above of course, it is a question of evolution there) but you can sink yourself below your proper level if you so desire, and you can again rise to your proper level.

Very well, then. You have a spirit dwelling in a spirit-body which has found its level – the phrase a 'natural station' was used, a happy one, I think – and we will imagine this spirit which is now dwelling upon his natural station and is therefore content, you will remark, because it *is* a natural station and because he feels that he is at home in the circumstances and in the conditions and so is content and happy. That is why the spirit-world, so-called, is a happy place because only those who can be happy there can *be* there: it is as simple as that. If you are not happy upon that spirit-plane you are not upon that spirit-plane – what more can I say? Therefore it is automatically and necessarily a happy place. Very well. This one remains upon the spirit-plane, undergoing experiences, or what you would regard as 'wasting time' if you wish, by failing to undergo experiences. It does not matter, for, as you have been told, there is no time to waste; time cannot be 'wasted', and so the spirit will remain in its state of happiness unless and until there comes a comprehension and understanding of the fact that yet greater happiness, greater possibilities, lie ahead and can be achieved by the exercise of thought, concentrated thought and desire – what you would refer to as spiritual advancement without a doubt – and so it is, for that is the process of spiritual advancement. It is not a question of intellectual learning, please do not misunderstand me in that respect. This process of spiritual advancement is as freely open to the ploughman or the charlady as to the scientist or the noble; it is not a matter of erudition. And then, when this spirit person begins to feel, not less happy, but to appreciate that even greater happiness and contentment are possible, then will come what you have referred to as the 'second death' – at his own will, at his own desire. He can refrain from the transition if he wishes for there may be a reason why he would prefer to remain below his *new* natural level – the new one to which he should aspire because he is ready for it – and I can give you there an example.

I will again refer you to our mutual friend the Keeper of our 'door', for he is and has been for some considerable time as far as the earth is concerned quite apt

77

and prepared and ready to make the transition into another state of being, but he prefers to remain as and where he is, for his own consolation, for his own contentment, to satisfy the urge within him, even though he is ready and apt to make the passing, but he is not compelled so to do. Now do you see the picture?

Chapter Eighteen

'ASTRAL-SHELLS'

Questioner. In your last talk upon the soul-body you left us to think over your statement that in some instances this body was retained beyond its normal use and became what might be known as an 'astral-shell'. The only conclusion we can come to is that such a soul-body is required for contact with the physical plane, because you give us to understand that Spirit can only contact the physical through a soul-body. Perhaps you could enlarge upon this point.

Abu. I cannot enlarge very far, for you have given me the reason at which I was sure you would arrive, but you have omitted an intermediate phase.

The prime purpose of retaining in being this 'astral-shell' as we will call it, is in the case where, as I postulated earlier, two persons living together on the spirit side of life in complete harmony and happiness and the one feeling the urge to rise to another plane, by mutual agreement the one is permitted or permits himself so to rise, leaving behind his partner. Now that one being bounden by the link of affection with the one who has necessarily for a little while been left behind, will be desirous of revisiting far more frequently the plane which he has just left than will the average person who has to a large degree severed the link because no real binding link existed. And so this astral-shell – 'hanging' as my son observed 'in the astral wardrobe!' – is kept in being and for this reason: that whilst the descending spirit coming from . . . shall we enumerate? . . . 'sphere three' down to 'sphere two', this descending spirit will not need the somewhat laborious process of accumulating and amalgamating the elements of 'plane two' in order to form another astral-body through which he can manifest. And so, for a time and only for a time (you will recall that my original words were 'for a time') this astral-shell may be kept in being by the thought power of the one who has passed on.

It will not be 'sentient', it will not be 'communicant' to the one left behind except when it shall be endowed with or reinformed with life by the spirit whose 'property' it is. Should there still remain a strong link with the earth-plane which we will designate 'sphere one' in this instance, then, as you rightly suggest, this same astral shell may be used for a descent on to 'plane one' in order that further communications may be made which would be of greater difficulty were this astral shell – this 'device' – not immediately available. It is a time and labour saving device and as such it is temporary only; it is for a time.

For, bethink you, sooner or later the link with the earth will dissolve – there will no longer be a link – and consequently no longer any need or desire to make further communication and, after a much longer time as you would regard time, the same will apply to the second plane and then of course – and probably before then but at least then – the shell will be released and it will dissolve into its particles as I have already explained to you. That is the purpose. You had quite evidently fully grasped that there could be a purpose and it is that.

To any objection that the descending spirit is perfectly capable of amalgamating and associating the material of the subsequent plane, the plane below, into *another* astral-body, my answer is: Yes indeed, with the expenditure of energy and power. If you know that you are going to use the body again within

79

a reasonable time, because the reason for such use still exists, then it would seem a little unnecessary, if not unwise, to demolish the link and be required to create a fresh one each and every time.

Questioner. There is only one thing that puzzles me. The astral-shell is maintained in being by some kind of effort or concentration of mental power by the spirit whose it was. Has that effort to be maintained in some way the whole time that this spirit is dwelling on some more remote sphere?

Abu. Have you got to keep your heart beating?

Questioner. I see. Then there is some kind of 'portion' of the spirit which can be allotted to that job without its involving any kind of 'drain' on the spirit?

Abu. It is no drain. The etheric-body will dissolve when the power which has sustained it, has held it together, is withdrawn, but you are not to think that whilst the informing spirit – on 'plane two' – is inhabiting his etheric-body that his thought and attention must be bent on the business of keeping his etheric-body together any more than your thought and attention are devoted to the holding together of your physical body. It is an analogous process.

Questioner. It is a natural function?

Abu. Thank you, it is a natural function. That will do usefully. And, just as you do not give a moment's thought to the beating of your heart, which must continue all the while your physical body is to live, so correspondingly when you come to dwell upon the spirit-plane you will not think of the spirit-body which you have, but upon departing from that plane to dwell in a yet higher sphere, if you shall then cease to think of that body because you have left it – if you shall then cease to think of that body at all – it shall dissolve. But if your intent was, as I have postulated, to make a return for a good enough reason – a reason good enough for yourself – if your intent is to return to the sphere which you are about to leave, the astral-body – the shell – will not so dissolve because your very intent will keep it together. It is not necessary to apply even a portion of the mind to the duty of holding it together, any more than it is necessary for you to give a moment's thought to the beating of your heart.

Questioner. It looks then as if the spirit mind, over there, has a something corresponding to what we call our 'subconscious mind' here.

Abu. Can you doubt it? I have claimed, as you know, and many religious teachers also have made the claim, that man is part of God. If you will follow that premise through logically, you will realise that man, as man, inhabiting a physical body, is not and cannot be part of a transcendental idea such as that which we have of God, *in one step*. Correspondingly, when you shed the physical body you dwell upon the plane of spirit in a more tenuous body – more tenuous that is to say to your present notions but not more tenuous to your mind when you shall find yourself there, for the succeeding stages do not become 'vaporous' to the individual concerned but 'vaporous' only to those who continue to dwell below them.

80

And so it goes on and on and on to infinity, and at *that* stage is God. And from there downwards there is God, in manifestation, in various forms, in varying forms. Man is God and God is man but not in one step only; down a chain, a stairway as it were, with an infinite number of steps. And so, upon the next stage of your existence of course, you have a 'something' as you have rightly said, comparable with your subconscious mind. Your present limited conditions make you aware of your conscious mind – necessarily, for reasons I have discussed in the past, aware of your *conscious* mind – and aware, a little doubtfully at times, that you may have a 'subconscious' mind; you admit the possibility.

When you shall 'dwell' as you would know it, in spirit, you will be aware of that subconscious mind with its greater content, and that subconscious mind will be aware that *it* has a subconscious mind! I dare not stop the process, for it does not stop. But it becomes, as you will appreciate, both more and more full and more and more rarefied and more and more 'holy', until it shall merge into the God-head and shall be all-inclusive, which it must be.

Questioner. There is one point which I have not yet raised: Can a spirit use any astral-shell, not necessarily the one which it created for itself? That question is based on the notion of these astral-shells 'hanging in a wardrobe'. I presume that it would be impossible for a spirit to use any other astral-shell than its own? Of course a spirit can occupy a physical body at the present time and I wondered if it was possible in the next sphere for the same sort of thing to happen.

2nd Questioner. You are suggesting a kind of 'obsession' of astral-shells?

Abu. Of course you are perfectly right; is it possible for another spirit to make use of the physical body belonging to someone else? I ask you, what is now happening *here*? And equally of course I am able to make this physical contact and to convert my thought – a little imperfectly without doubt – but to convert my thought into speech in order that it may reach your ears through the medium of an astral-body, an 'astral-shell' – the shell in fact belonging to the instrument whom I now use – necessarily I am using the astral-shell, the body of the spirit who is my instrument. Indeed, and that process continues quite a long way up the scale.

Questioner. It is true then that any of these astral-shells could be used by any other spirit?

Abu. With approval and with permission of the spirit, my son; that follows automatically; for of course this hypothetical person (spirit) who has advanced from 'sphere two' to 'sphere three' and has left behind deliberately and intentionally the form of an astral or etheric-body for his own use, will be aware of that astral-shell should anything occur to it or threaten to occur to it and, should someone perhaps – I believe you have a phrase 'personating' or 'impersonating' spirit – should one such endeavour to make use of the astral-shell belonging to the spirit now safely 'tucked away' in 'sphere three', he will immediately dematerialise that shell. And so, without permission or approval, it cannot be done, but with such permission and approval, why not, indeed?

In point of fact there would of course be no conflict of such a nature in any sphere of reasonable spiritual advancement but it might occur a little further down the scale.

Questioner. It can occur on our plane in the form of obsession?

Abu. You have seized upon the point. The circumstances parallel themselves all the way as far as I am aware. I am fully prepared to learn that at some stage I shall cease to be even Abu, even in the position of a father who wishes to bring a little teaching if possible to his children – I am prepared to accept that it may be so. I can only say that as far as my experience goes it has not yet been so and as far ahead as I am able to see it will not be so. For the individuality – not the personality you will remember – the individuality persists and continues to persist as far as I have been able to see and to envisage and as far as my enquiry goes, and, whilst my own status is not a very high one, at the same time my enquiries have been pushed to a considerable distance.

For, as you will appreciate, I am at least as interested in my own future as you are in yours. You will not make the mistake of thinking that Abu is any the less human because he lives 'in the fourth heaven'! We are human, my children, because we are part of *this* experiment. It may be, as I have said, that later on we may merge with the results – the resultants – of yet other experiments and at such a junction I cannot know what may take place, but as far as my experience goes and as far as my enquiry goes, we who have commenced our individualisation as what you know as human beings, will remain human beings until the purpose is fully served – and there again we enter into the inscrutable regions – but it will be what you would know as a very long time and it will be what I too shall recognise as a very long time. But do not make the mistake of thinking that we do not remain human indeed – purged, I trust, purged and cleansed a little, with the eyes a little wider open, with perhaps slightly greater comprehension, because of our more fortunate circumstances, of the love of God, of the necessity of appreciating and responding to that love – yes, by all means – but we are still human and happy that it should be so.

For, with respect to other orders of creation – and there are such – none among them can understand, can sympathise, can be compassionate with, humanity as can those who have themselves been human and remain so.

You have the story of the God who became man upon your earth-plane, and, as a parable, it is perfect. For the God who is God *must* know of the life which his human children are living and are to live, otherwise He could not know of their troubles, of their difficulties, of their trials, and so the God who became man (but not necessarily in the manner in which it has been described), the God who became man is as necessary as the man who shall be God.

And so, the blessing which I know to be outflowing from that fount of all love and of blessing and warmth towards us, towards me, towards you, towards all the children, be they upon a high plane of spiritual advancement or upon the lowest, be their intellects magnificent ones or be they merely 'vegetable' – the love and the blessing and the warmth alike flow out towards all.

Man, whatever his standing, whatever his status, has merely to appreciate *that* fact and to respond to it, and his advancement in spiritual terms is assured.

And with that thought I will leave you for a little while.

Chapter Nineteen

THE EMPLOYMENT OF THE ETHERIC-BODY IN "CONTROL"

Questioner. We raised the question recently of a spirit occupying a soul-body or astral-shell other than its own and you stated that this was possible with the consent of the owning spirit. This is an interesting point. I had previously been of the opinion that to control a medium it was necessary for his soul-body to vacate the physical body and for the controlling personality to substitute his own soul-body and spirit. Perhaps you could explain this to us.

Abu. It is a little difficult, as perhaps you will appreciate, for me to give you a clear view of mechanistic matters such as this because it is necessary for me to speak in earthly terms and because the picture that must be drawn within your mind upon hearing my words will necessarily create itself in well-nigh earthly terms, whereas in fact, of course, all the things that I have told you and that I shall tell you regarding the spirit-body, the astral-body (we have numerous names for it) must be regarded as something in the nature of an analogy. For, when I have claimed, as I do claim, that the spirit-body is a material one in that it is substantial, you must necessarily think of a physical, earthly, material substance whilst being all too fully aware that the spirit-body is *not* composed of earthly substance, and therefore my claim that it is substantial insists upon being something in the nature of an analogy, since you cannot conceive of a non-physical material, and so the picture must be a little confused.

But the general principle or method of control, of the use of the physical organism of a medium, in the manner in which I myself am now performing it, is substantially the same no matter who the controller and the instrument may be whenever what you know as 'deep trance' is involved, that is to say where the personality of the medium is withdrawn to the greatest possible degree. You will remark, in parenthesis, that it is not entirely and completely withdrawn for always and ever there must remain a link.

Should some danger threaten, the medium's own spirit-self will be recalled – it will be aware of the fact – it will be recalled immediately to take charge of the physical organism; and where strong emotions are brought into question the same thing will apply to such a degree, as I am sure you are aware, that the controlling, communicating spirit may be ejected quite suddenly and unexpectedly. That is the deep trance condition and that is the normal method of control where deep trance is used – where the personality of the communicating spirit is able to manifest with the least interference, shall I say, from the 'subconscious content' of the medium. But in all cases the etheric-body or astral-shell of the individual concerned must be used in order to inform, to 'manipulate', to cause to work, the physical body.

The *spirit* or astral-body to which we are referring is indissolubly linked with the physical: when that link shall be broken the physical body is what you call 'dead'; it is no longer possible for it to be informed by spirit once that link, that cord is broken, and consequently there is an astral-shell appropriate to the physical vessel which is indissolubly linked therewith and it is not possible to substitute for that astral-shell *another* and to link it similarly so that you have a kind of 'Siamese-twin' effect: that cannot be done. Therefore it is necessary for a spirit wishing to communicate in this manner to make use of the astral-shell or etheric-body of the medium which the communicating spirit will proceed to inform and which, by automatic repercussion will operate, will 'manipulate' the physical body just as does the same etheric-body when it is instructed by the spirit of the medium himself.

The *spirit* of the medium can detach itself from its etheric or astral-body without interference, without distress, without trouble, and that astral-shell can be occupied and taken charge of, as it were, by a spirit wishful to communicate, but it is the same astral-body or shell all the time. You will of course be aware that, as I have just said, the spirit can detach itself without bother or distress from the astral-shell for you will recall our 'astral wardrobe'. Quite evidently the spirit has not suffered from leaving behind the astral-body and quite evidently the astral-body, in that case no longer imbued with life, no longer informed by life, whilst it does remain, as we have already suggested, held together and 'crystallised', has not changed; it does not alter. Neither party to the affair will suffer distress or anything of the kind.

But that is the essential point – to each physical body there is an etheric-body which was created at the same time and at the same rate as the physical and its purpose is to *animate* the physical and the link is indissoluble whilst life in the physical is to continue; but that is not to say that the *spirit* is *constrained* into that astral-shell: the constraint is between two modes of material – the spirit mode and the physical, earthly mode.

Questioner. I had apparently been misled in this matter for I had always understood that, in the control of a physical body, the astral-body 'stepped out' and allowed the controlling entity to take charge. As a matter of fact I have heard it said by so-called clairvoyants that they could see the astral-body of the person under control alongside the body of that person whilst under control. I now see that that could not be possible.

Abu. Yes that is perfectly possible, and my explanation of the original facts contains within it the explanation of the phenomenon to which you refer. For, bethink you, the communicating spirit – perhaps not I myself but we will suppose one dwelling normally upon the next stage or phase – a dear one perhaps very recently passed over – that one will be inhabiting or informing an etheric-body and that one will wish to communicate. His spirit will, because it can, detach itself from the etheric-body which *it* is using on the spirit plate of life and it will enter into the etheric-body of the medium (still linked with the physical), this etheric-body having been vacated by the spirit power of the medium, and it will proceed to animate the physical body of the medium and your clairvoyant will see the etheric-body of the *medium* being used by the communicating spirit and the etheric-body or that spirit, not at the moment in use at all, 'standing by', waiting for its owner to inform it with the necessary life.

Questioner. I had, apparently, been misled by the clairvoyant who thought it was the etheric-body of the medium which he saw alongside whereas in fact it was the etheric-body of the person communicating. I see now how the mistake arose.

Abu. That, is the position and if you shall ask one who is sensitive – a clairvoyant is your word – if you can question one such on getting into touch with the dwellers in spirit, you would learn that to the dwellers – the permanent dwellers – on the spirit-plane, their compeers are as real, as solid and as substantial as they are themselves. It is *life* in a word – it is life largely as you know it in terms of sentience, in terms of vision, of sound and hearing but the *spirit* (not the spirit-body but the spirit) of a medium such as the person whose body I am now using, whilst still living, and aware in the greater mind, of experience which he is undergoing whilst temporarily in the spirit world and temporarily denuded of the etheric-body – that spirit will appear to be a 'ghost', as it were, to the dwellers upon the spirit-plane. For the manifestation of the *spirit* of the medium in this particular instance and in other such instances is of a more tenuous nature than is the true manifestation through the astral or etheric-body which is your lot and your right when you shall come here to dwell.

And it is largely for that reason that the medium so very seldom brings back to his etheric-body and therefore to his physical brain any real recollection of events which he has taken part in, events which have transpired whilst he has been out of the body. Because the material which it is necessary to . . . what is the word? . . . to 'manipulate' – it is a clumsy word . . . in order that memory, recollection and appreciation shall be available, is no longer with him; he has voluntarily left it behind, do you see, so that whilst he is conscious and aware at the time of what is going on, he has nothing upon which to impress a memory. That is the difficulty. When it is necessary for a dweller upon a further plane, such as myself for instance, to descend the range of vibrations and take up my being for a time upon the plane next to your earth, then I will necessarily adopt an etheric-shell in order that I may be seen and heard – known and felt – of the dwellers upon that plane. And similarly, if I am to communicate with my dear friends upon earth, I must adopt a body which I borrow for that purpose.

It is a parallel. The 'I' who descends from the 'fourth heaven' to the plane lying immediately next to your world of earth is a 'ghost' to the dwellers *there*. I use the word in a reasonable sense, for they would not be able to see or hear me clearly – as somewhat shadowy, yes. And for the time being, the spirit of my present medium – the person who I am using – is functioning as a 'ghost'.

Questioner. We are all ghosts to each other in a different vibration?

Abu. That is precisely the case and if you will recall that thought and bear it in mind you will be able to unravel a number of things which might otherwise be difficulties.

Chapter Twenty

SOUL AND SPIRIT – INCARNATION

Questioner. What is the difference between soul and spirit?

Abu. The difference between soul and spirit is in the first instance a difference in the pronunciation of words, for, before we can commence to discuss the difference, if difference exists, we must be clear as to what is meant by the use of those earthly words. It is pointless and futile for me to attempt to lay down the law in respect of the nature of the soul or the nature of the spirit unless and until we shall have arrived at agreement as to what we mean by those terms.

I would therefore take the word soul which you have used and translate it, I hope correctly, by using a term which I believe to be Greek, which is the 'psyche' – you will correct me if I am wrong in this respect.

Questioner. There is certainly a Greek word 'psyche' but as to whether it has the same meaning for people now as the word 'soul' I cannot be sure.

Abu. I offer you my own definition of these terms; not that it is a unique definition or that my definition has greater validity than any other but simply and solely for the reasons which I have already expressed, namely that we must be in agreement. And since throughout the course of our discussions I have always used the term 'spirit' to indicate the fundamental essence (be it undifferentiated or be it individualised is of no material moment) I prefer to make use of the word 'soul' in the sense of the 'psyche'; from which will stem, as you will see, faculties which you know as 'psychic' (but not necessarily spiritual) and then we shall be upon common ground when endeavouring to discuss any difference.

Questioner. I think that the idea in my mind was that the soul was something which contains the spirit in the same way as the physical body contains the two during the earth life, but what I cannot quite grasp is – when the soul enters the physical body and the spirit enters the physical body. Is it a simultaneous happening or is it the fact that, as some schools of thought believe, the spirit does not enter the body until after the soul?

Abu. It were unkind if I were to say that you are totally wrong in the whole conception.

Questioner. That of course is what I want to know. It is a line of thought – I did not say it was mine.

Abu. I thank you. The falsity in the first premise which you laid down lies in your use of the word, perhaps a little carelessly, 'contains', for after all we have spoken of together, you cannot suppose that a physical body can *contain* spirit. Neither can or does the physical body contain the soul or psyche, but the three (for it is a form of trinity as you will observe) are in a close association and the

86

psyche or soul-body is more closely associated with the physical body than is the spirit, for the spirit is never contained; it manifests through different bodies be it the psyche (or the soul-body) or be it the physical body which itself is operated upon by the psyche, the two bodies, coincidentally as it were, being informed by the power of spirit, not *containing* that spirit. Neither must you envisage the spirit as an aura surrounding the physical body or the psychic body – the 'soul' that is to say, under the terminology that we are now using. Because the spirit is not existent within your time and space. It impinges thereupon and it uses as a means – as a medium – for such impingement, the soul or psychic body (it has other names). But the soul, so-called, is the link between the essentially material physical body and the quite essentially non-material spirit, and that process continues.

You posed a supplementary question as to whether of the two, the soul or the spirit – the psychic body or the spirit – entered into possession, as it were, of the physical body the one before the other or the other before the one. No such question arises. As to the time of such union, for it is well-nigh a union – there is a strong linking between the psyche and the physical body, although that union is still a tenuous one in that under certain circumstances the soul, the psyche, the astral-body, can leave or depart from the physical retaining only sufficient 'grip', as it were, of the situation as to enable the physical body to live at all, but the linkage is otherwise firm, much firmer than the bond between spirit and either body.

For the spirit is not *constrained*, whereas the psyche, whilst the physical body is in a condition to live, is so constrained and must remain associated with the physical body even whilst disassociating itself at times, during sleep for example or during periods of unconsciousness due perhaps to injury – whilst it disassociates itself to a large degree, none the less it is still conjoined therewith and linked thereto and the link may not be broken without the death of the physical body supervening. But the spirit is not constrained. That is the essence of the point that I would make.

Questioner. Does not the spirit enter at the moment of conception?

Abu. It is a little later than the moment of conception. I become intensely biological at this point! A little later than the moment of conception a process occurs in the body of the woman who is to be the vehicle for bearing the child that is to be born, a process which is known as 'adhesion', when the fertilised ovum becomes attached to the body of the woman. Then and then only does the spirit commence to 'form', simultaneously with the accretion, the aggregation of cells of the physical body – simultaneously with that process the spirit power, which has already entered into association with the hypothetical child which is to be, that spirit proceeds to build a soul-body simultaneously with the physical body for the reason that this same spirit which is to manifest (for reasons into which we will not delve for no such delving is possible as we have already decided) upon the material plane of earth must create a physical body in order that the spirit may so manifest. And since upon the wearing out or using up or the destruction by injury of that physical body the spirit will still be required to continue to manifest upon what you know as the spirit-planes, it will require a further body of manifestation and so the two bodies of manifestation are builded simultaneously by the same power of spirit which operates upon the physical through the medium of the soul or psychic body, which is of a more tenuous and finer order of vibration than is the physical. The process once commenced will continue, subject of course, to accidental happenings upon the earth-plane which may cut short the intention.

I will not trouble you with analogies, but again I will emphasise, for I must emphasise, the thought which I have already placed before you – that spirit cannot be constrained. For, as I have already said, all spirit is of the same essence – it is the God essence. All spirit is God; that is not to say that God is only what you and we know as 'spirit'. God is, God may be, almost certainly more than we can know, but such as we can know is of God and the spirit which, from being undifferentiated, shall be 'crystallised' out with the intent that it shall individualise by undergoing experiences upon the earth-plane and subsequently upon the spirit-planes, that spirit too is as much a part of God as is the God-head himself, and so that spirit cannot be constrained.

It will operate, it does operate because it must, but it is not compelled, it is not constrained by any factor or any feature of existence of a lower order than itself. That is the one point that I must keep always before you. All spirit is of the fundamental essence: there is not dark spirit and light spirit – some coloured and some clear. Spirit is spirit and spirit is God and God is spirit, and I will ask you to bear that in mind when we are speaking of spirit as such.

In looseness of phraseology we frequently permit ourselves to speak of *the* spirit of a man when we really mean what we have been describing this evening as the soul-body. It is a simple matter to refer to the soul-body as *the* spirit and the spirit as informing the soul-body, but no *body* is spirit: spirit is beyond all bodily content.

Questioner. It is confusing to liken spirit to ether, as we did in one or our previous talks, because I think it is possible to have 'contained ether' or what you might term 'bound ether' and possibly that has misled me into thinking that spirit could be bound in some way.

Abu. Your analogy is perfect but do not confuse any semi-physical 'ether', of science, with its term of 'bound ether', as representing for example matter in your world – do not confuse that with the all-pervading spirit in respect of which I accepted your term 'ether'. I had no intention at all that confusion should arise within your mind. But the analogy is perfect, for individualised spirit – what I have referred to, for I could not find other words, as a 'portion' of spirit, is in effect bound spirit, like unto your bound ether and related to the undifferentiated spirit as is the bound ether related to the undifferentiated ether. But they are not identical; they are not to be identified, because spirit cannot be bound *into* matter, whereas the suggestion of the scientist that 'bound ether' is matter, or to put it the other way round that matter is nothing but bound ether, is a hypothesis and only a hypothesis. Whereas the all-pervading spirit is not *manifest* upon your world; it cannot manifest *itself*. Its effects can be made manifest among you through the medium of the bodies which it shall wear and inform, but in itself spirit is not detectable by anything other than spirit.

I hope that will resolve your difficulty.

Chapter Twenty-One

HAS AN INCARNATING SPIRIT CHOICE OF ITS VEHICLE?

Questioner. There is an idea which is sometimes put forward, ostensibly by persons from your side of life, to the effect that the spirits of men, on entering the physical envelope at birth, have the power of choice as to what body they shall inform or inhabit. What amount of truth would you say there is in such an assertion?

Abu. It is going to be a little difficult to answer. The assertion to which you refer is made usually, I believe, in connection with a certain body of teaching which expresses the view that man – the spirit of man incarnate upon the earth-plane – has a "fate", a "karma" is the word, which must be "worked out" and the suggestion is therefore made that the spirit has a choice of the bodily envelope which it shall inform and inhabit in order that it may the better "work out" this "karma".

I can venture no more than an opinion; as you will be aware, I prefer not to dogmatise. We have spoken of the subject of reincarnation which is linked closely with this same matter to which you now refer. I am merely clearing the ground in order that we shall all of us have a clear view as to the reason for the assertion which is made. Reincarnation we have dealt with to a degree and there I have preferred not to dogmatise. I do not say it is impossible. I have said that, in certain circumstances, in certain instances, it is not only possible but that it does occur. I can go no further than that in respect of the present assertion. But, I am not prepared to support the view of those who claim that "karma" is all-important, that it carries with it the load of "sin" (that, I suppose, might be the word) resulting from previous incarnations and that *therefore* the spirit has a choice as to which physical vessel it shall inhabit.

Because, unless there were sound reasons – a reason, at least – there would seem to be little point in the spirit exercising a choice, in any event. That is why I have had to introduce the allied and twin aspects of karma and reincarnation. Reincarnation is, necessarily, the basis of the whole suggestion.

But, again, I will not dogmatise. I cannot say "This does *not* occur", because, although not within my knowledge, or seldom, within my knowledge, it does not occur in general terms. Here and there, yes: a choice is made, deliberately, voluntarily and for a purpose and for a reason, but, in general, no.

For, you touch – perhaps you do not realise it – but you touch upon a far more basic and fundamental thing than the mere choice by the spirit of a physical vessel. For, such a suggestion would indicate that the choosing spirit is already fully developed and has its powers and that it merely exercises a choice of the physical vessel. But that is not always the case. The spirit of man becomes individualised in the becoming of the man. It is not an adult and fully-grown and developed spirit which crams itself into the foetus in pre-natal moments and thereafter struggles against an environment which is much too small for it until the child shall have grown to stature. That is not the case at all; the very idea is something of an absurdity, as you will appreciate. No, it is not so. I cannot say, in the first instance – I may not say – *the* spirit chooses *the* body because there is not *the* spirit at that point and at that moment. There is but *"Spirit"*, and spirit in general, broad terms, the essential "spirit" of which we have spoken – and a "portion" – if one may designate it as a portion – a "portion" of spirit will enter within the vessel which is to be born in the usual way and to inhabit your earth-plane. It is not a happy description for it is not a portion of spirit as if "sliced off with a knife". It is extremely difficult to give you a view.

You can understand that the spirit which has now associated itself with the vehicle which is to be born, to develop and to expand by the aggregation of matter and cells, that spirit itself evolves and develops and individualises *during* the becoming of the man. Therefore, and this of course touches again upon the question of reincarnation, generally speaking, there is no question of a choice being exercised, for there is no thinking, developed mind which could make a choice in the first instance. In the event – the reasonably rare event – of a reincarnation such as we have discussed in the past – then, yes, a choice is made.

We have instanced saint-like men who have returned to your earth-plane quite deliberately and voluntarily, perhaps more than once. Quite obviously there would be no point in their attempted return, their successful return, unless they were able to make a choice which would permit *them* to do the work for which they had chosen to return to the earth-plane. Therefore, in such cases, yes, there is a choice. In other cases there is nothing to choose.

There are those – (there is a body of teaching which has a great deal of light behind it without a doubt) there are those amongst the adherents to such a "sect", a "cult" – I do not know what to call it – who have a tendency to generalise to too great a degree. They will, perhaps, receive information of, for example, *a* reincarnation, which may perhaps be substantiated reasonably, and it may in fact have been a true case of reincarnation, and, from that, these people will proceed to argue from the particular to the general and make the claim that men reincarnate upon the earth-plane time after time, and, since they must seek a reason for such an absurdity, they introduce the almost equally absurd notion of "karma".

I wish that I could give you a clearer idea, in your terms, of the matter – namely, the oneness of spirit descending, parting itself off from the parent body, as it were, informing and inhabiting a physical vessel which is being created by spirit – not by *a* spirit – but by Spirit – and, thereafter, that (again I must use the word) "portion" of spirit taking charge, as it were, of that tiny vessel and regulating its growth, its evolution, its development, and the spirit "becoming" as the man becomes.

Chapter Twenty-Two

THE "POOL" OF SPIRIT

Questioner. Does a new spirit choose its parents? I suppose there is a kind of 'pool of spirit' from which it comes when it is to be incarnated upon the earth and I wondered if it could exercise choice in that incarnation.

Abu. For the first part of your question as to whether a 'new incarnation', if I may call it so, exercises choice in the matter of parents, I have already spoken upon that matter and I have denied that any such choice is exercised for the very simple reason that there is no personality, no individuality which *could* exercise such a choice and therefore the second part of your question is virtually an answer to the first. For the assumption that you make therein, namely that newly incarnated spirit is, as it were, drawn from a 'pool' of spirit, is in a large measure correct, and that I think, very shortly answers your question in both halves.

But I imagine that you will wish me to proceed a little further, because I am aware that the picture which you have drawn and to which I have acceded, the picture of a pool of Spirit from which a 'portion' is withdrawn for the purpose of incarnating in a human body, a fleshly body, must be an extremely difficult one for you to grasp, for you will wish to know who determines what portion – what 'size of portion' – of spirit, (I put it in very earthy terms and the words have in fact no meaning when applied to spirit) but you will ask the question: Who and what determines which portion of Spirit shall next incarnate and into which vehicle? It is not like that. I shall have extreme difficulty I fear in giving you a picture which you can grasp, particularly because, a little later on, when we meet on a future occasion, you are going to speak to me about an extremely difficult subject upon which I touched, over-hastily, namely the 'Golden Age', and when I give you a reply in respect of that question it will leave you far more bewildered than perhaps you are at present. And so the purpose of my answering your questions will have been lost, for I shall give you no information which you can absorb. But I have already warned you of that.

To revert to this present difficulty of the 'pool of spirit'; I must say this, and hope that you can find sufficient commonsense in my words for them to have meaning for you. Your difficulty lies primarily in the fact, I feel reasonably sure, that you are thinking of a pool of spirit as if it were a pool of water, contained in and confined by something, somewhere other than upon your earth – to wit, in the 'next world' – which it is quite usual for earth dwellers to understand as lying 'above' the earth's surface. If you have a concept such as that then of course quite obviously you will have the greatest of difficulty in understanding the picture which I have endeavoured to draw (your own picture, in fact) of the pool of spirit from which a portion is withdrawn. For a picture of that nature is far too earthy; the analogy is far from perfect. It is horribly imperfect, in fact, for it bears no relationship at all to the facts.

The facts, if you can grasp them as facts, are these. Your planet, the earth, with the dwellers thereupon, is permeated throughout with spirit essence (it is a convenient word which I have come across). This spirit essence is coexistent with your world and, whilst it does not occupy physical space in that you cannot take a pint pot and fill it with spirit essence, neither can you measure off one foot or one yard square or cubic content of spirit essence and box it up and send it as a parcel – whilst this spirit essence does not occupy space – it is none the less *of* space – if that phrase shall have meaning for you.

I hesitate to leave what is perhaps more my own field and to trespass upon a field which is most certainly not mine, but I feel impelled to do so. I will assume that you have a certain amount of scientific knowledge and I will refer you to the findings of your scientists in recent years as to the composition of your matter as you know it upon the earth, the solid matter which is 'indestructible' and 'unchangeable' except in so far as it can be converted from one form into another. That solid matter has, by the mental activities of your scientists, been reduced to a large amount of empty space and, within that space, a few small magnetic charges. (I cannot be very precise, I do not know all the terms, but I endeavour to give you the scientific picture as I have been given it).

Now, the space within that atom of matter is empty space: there is nothing therein. The matter is comprised of or comprised by electro-magnetic charges which have an effect. More than that cannot be said. Matter is something which has an 'effect' upon other matter and also upon spirit, but it has an effect upon spirit, not by virtue of the electro-magnetic charges, but by virtue of the spirit essence which in fact permeates the empty space which comprises by far the larger part of the material atom.

It is impalpable; it is intangible; you cannot sense it in any way. You cannot measure it, you cannot see it, and I claim that it is there: I can but 'claim' that it is there. And so, as I have said, the essence of spirit – of all Spirit – (it is a part, if you will, of God, for God comprises all spirit), this 'portion' (again I must use the word – it is not a happy one but I must use it) this portion of spirit which is as it were allocated to your earthly plane, is coexistent with that earthly plane and permeates all things. And, when a spirit is to individualise – is to 'become' – upon the earth-plane a man, a creature, an animal, a plant (it matters not, the differences are differences of degree only, not of kind) when the manifestation of life is to be brought into being upon the earth-plane and an act is performed which you know as conception, the spirit does not have to *come* from somewhere, enter into somewhere by some pathway and seize upon the cells which are eventually, under the guidance of that same spirit, to aggregate and to grow and to become a man. The spirit does not have to do any of those things for the spirit already permeates the whole of the space, including the bodies of the father and the mother, the seed which is to be the tree, and everything else which (again for inscrutable reasons) the Creator has decided shall manifest Himself in life. Does that make your question a little clearer perhaps or does it obscure it even more?

Questioner. I think it makes it much clearer. I admit that previously I had some vague conception of a 'pool' of spirit 'away' from here which was drawn upon but I now see that spirit permeates what we commonly know as 'ether' and therefore can be easily drawn upon since it is there to begin with.

Abu. I thank you for that word. It was the word which I would have used had I been able to call it to mind, for what I have called 'spirit essence', in perhaps a

92

semi-religious mode of speech, could more scientifically perhaps be referred to as ether, for the ether of which you speak has no *material* existence; it will not be 'discovered' by your scientists. It may be postulated; it has, in fact, been postulated as a necessity for explaining certain phenomena, but it has no material existence. It will not affect your instruments, your material instruments, and so what I have referred to semi-religiously as the 'spirit essence' can be referred to scientifically as ether and that is all-permeating and all-pervasive and it is ever present. It is quite unaffected and cannot be affected by the things of the material world for it is upon a different range of frequency, a different 'vibration', and therefore it – that is to say the spirit, and that is to say the ether, is not apparent to you whose spirit (your 'portion' of the ether) has necessarily been 'cloaked' down. I have referred to this matter before. The spirit essence then is not apparent to you until it shall become manifest by interacting with the electric or electromagnetic charges which it, the spirit essence, combines and aggregates and directs to form what you know as matter, when that matter is to become a living body.

May I give you a little analogy which might perhaps be of assistance although I fear that you will have to use your imaginations. I will ask you to imagine a large sea of water, or perhaps a large tank of water and a fish, with intelligence such as a man's, swimming about therein.

Whilst the fish swims peacefully about therein he is not aware of the water as such; the water as such means nothing to him, it is his medium of existence and to a large degree it permeates his body. He swallows the water and takes it in; it is, as it were, part of himself and so he is not really aware of the water as such. Perhaps he may poke his nose above the surface of the water if he is a very wise fish and become aware of the greater, freer atmosphere of air above the water – yes, that is so. But now I will ask your imagination to function, if you will permit it, and I will suggest that within the body of the water wherein this fish is swimming so peacefully about his affairs, suddenly, by some scientific means perhaps, certain portions of the water become frozen into cubes of ice. The fish is then aware – for he will bump his nose into the ice cube – that there is something there – to wit, a cube of ice – which was not there before, and he will imagine, as you have imagined, that this cube of ice has been miraculously drawn down from a sphere above and plunged into his pool of water.

Not so; it is the essence of the water but materialised into a form appreciable by the intelligence of the fish. So with spirit essence, or ether if you prefer the term, you are correspondingly not aware of it; you cannot be aware of it unless and until it shall impact upon you a little super-normally shall we say, as in this *present* instance when you have mental contacts with it and when I have the privilege of using a 'crystallised' body in order that I make my speech apparent to your physical ears. But otherwise you will not be aware of the ocean of spirit in which you move and which moves with you though you become so aware when you see that a child is born for you know that that child, shall we say, contains a 'portion' of spirit – (it is not a happy phrase but it will do). Does that help at all?

Questioner. Yes, it seems an excellent analogy and put in a simple form.

Abu. That is very pleasing for I am always happy if I can give a picture in earthly words of happenings which are 'unearthly'. It is a subject of great interest without a doubt and we who wish to turn the minds of men towards the love of God in order that their progress both upon earth and after their sojourn upon earth shall be made more happy and more speedy towards the source of the Love – we are always glad when a little light, even upon such a matter as this which is of no *fundamental* importance quite obviously, since it deals with a temporal and temporary state of affairs, can be shed, and so I am glad that my words have meaning for you.

Chapter Twenty-Three

REINCARNATION

Questioner. There is a great deal of talk about "reincarnation" and it is even supposed by many people to be of an "automatic" nature. Such experience as we have of those who have left our world for spirit-life seems not to bear this out in any way. Whilst we, here, do not feel that this is in any sense a vital problem, we think it must be of interest on both sides of life and we should welcome anything you can tell us about it.

Abu. It is an extremely controversial question. I myself have no knowledge whatever of any soul who has been in any way *compelled* to re-incarnate upon your earth-plane but I *have* knowledge of spirit-persons who have deliberately incarnated yet again for specific purposes of their own, but, generally speaking, not for personal advancement, for personal gain, but with the object of doing just the work which my band of brothers and I myself endeavour to do in *this* manner. For example (though perhaps I should not mention personalities – yet it can do no harm) there is a man of whom you have knowledge, who is dwelling in the Dark Continent and who is doing a wonderful work.

Questioner. I feel sure I know to whom you refer.

Abu. That man is a reincarnation of a being – a person – who has dwelt upon your earth-plane, not once before, but several times. There is a purity, a refinement, in the spirit informing and inhabiting this particular man at the moment which has been refined by passing through the fire many times, always with the intent and purpose of assisting, of aiding, of helping, of educating fellowmen on each and every occasion.

In that sense I will give this matter of reincarnation my "blessing". When such a thing can happen, as it can, then, quite evidently, it falls in line with the will of the Divine Power, whose one wish and thought is to express to you – to us, to all – His Love.

If it can be achieved – in the opinion of the individual spirit – if it can be better achieved by incarnation – a dwelling again in the flesh – then that is permitted.

But, whilst I do not positively deny, I cannot affirm that anything at all in the nature of compulsory reincarnation exists. *I* have never been so compelled. I have never felt any such compulsion and I know of none who has. But, within the limits that I have mentioned, I must say that such a thing is *possible*.

Questioner. In view of that I must say that I feel the possibilities of self-deception among people here on earth must be enormous, because there are many thousands of people who have persuaded themselves that there is some kind of automatic reincarnation – even, in the view of certain people, an immediate reincarnation following upon death.

It has always offended our reason and I am very glad to have your information and experience on the matter.

Abu. I think such a thesis would offend the reason of any thinking man – on many grounds, into which I will not go: they are familiar to you. But I would say one other thing on this point. You say that there are many people upon the earth-plane who deceive themselves (I think those were your words) in this respect. I would remind you that on a previous occasion (when I dealt as well as I was able with the matter), the question of the *minds* – conscious and subconscious etc. arose when I made it as clear as I could that there are not many minds but one, and yet, none the less, that this one mind can be and is in fact in contact with both the material and the spirit planes at the same time and it is a question of attention rather than of transference in terms of position that matters – these people who, as you say, delude themselves – their thinking, conscious minds – into this idea of a compulsory reincarnation, also have a mind which is in contact with spirit as well as with the material plane, and confusion may exist – confusion may become apparent – when the aspect of the mind, the "attention" of the mind, which is directed to spirit, endeavours to bring into the conscious mind, which is dealing with matters of the earth-plane, things which the conscious mind cannot grasp because it must work through brain.

It is not a conscious delusion; it is not an intentional self-deception, in so far as one part of the mind is endeavouring to convey to another but more limited part of the mind information which this limited mind cannnot fully grasp and accept, and distortion frequently does occur, giving rise to delusions.

There is one further point: that the conscious mind of the person being so deluded – self-deluded – this conscious mind is fully aware that the information which it imagines it has seized upon fully and accurately comes from the spirit side of life and therefore it has an authority which it should not really carry. But, it has that authority for the individual because he is aware that these ideas come from outside and beyond his conscious mind. Therefore he is not infrequently left under the impression that he is receiving some sort of transcendental guidance from knowledgeable spirit-people in respect of these matters – whereas in fact, it is just a jumble of ideas conveyed imperfectly to his conscious mind by his own "sub-conscious" mind.

Chapter Twenty-Four

MORE ON REINCARNATION

Questioner. It is suggested by a 'pupil' of yours that reincarnation, although it need not be compulsory, is a means by which we can still learn something in this earth-life. From your teachings, we learn that progress can be made in practically every direction in the next sphere of life and there is no necessity for anybody to come back here, to learn. Can you clarify that point?

Abu. I can indeed, and I shall be happy to do so. The points of view are not in opposition but can swiftly and easily be reconciled. Or course my 'pupil' as you have termed him, is in the right when he claims that in the case of a reincarnation, a voluntary, intentional reincarnation, the spirit reincarnating can *learn*. Are you not all spirit, here, now and always, and is not spirit always open for learning, for instruction, for the acquisition of knowledge, of wisdom and of spiritual advancement, in whatever conditions? But certainly; I would not exclude the earth-plane, for the earth-plane is only *secondarily* a plane of physical manifestation; it is primarily a plane of spirit manifestation, just as much as is what you have learned to call the next world; for it is but one world, and the spirit can learn whilst upon the earth-plane as effectively as it can learn hereafter, but not necessarily *more* so.

That is the rock upon which the upholders of the theory of reincarnation usually strike, for they usually, as I gather, will make the claim that it is *necessary* for the spirit to return from the spirit world to a further reincarnation upon the physical plane in order that it may learn, it being suggested that no learning, no acquisition is possible elsewhere than upon the earth-plane; and that is quite wrong. But that does not exclude the possibility of learning whilst in spirit upon earth, for that goes on of course. But having shed the physical envelope, having garnered such knowledge, such learning, as may have been garnered during a sojourn upon earth, the spirit will then continue – (it will not recommence, there is no interuption) – it will continue to exist, functioning and manifesting in a body of a different vibration wave-length and still learning, and so and so and so on; there is no difference. And if there shall be, for an express purpose, an intense desire to return to the earth-plane, as I have stated in the past that is permissible, by consultation with and with the approval of the Great Ones.

The matter is disposed of, if I may put it in such a way, once and for all by our "loving God", who has made the necessary dispositions that such a thing may take place, but it is within the discretion of the Great Ones whose attention is primarily directed towards your earth-plane, whether a reincarnation shall be permitted or not; it is not solely and purely at the discretion of the individual spirit person, and you would not expect it to be so. For there are many unworthy ones, many lowly ones of poor advancement, who would most gladly exchange their spirit conditions for a renewal of the earth conditions which once they knew. They would in effect most gladly reincarnate were it possible, for whilst upon the earth-plane they can apparently (since the physical appears to transcend the spiritual), set aside conditions which in the spirit will afflict them grievously; but that is not permitted, and so that is why I have qualified my remarks by stating that a voluntary reincarnation must receive the approval of the Great Ones.

The personal desire is the deciding factor in that if you do not wish to reincarnate you are not compelled so to do, but if you do wish to reincarnate it must be for a desirable and a worthy purpose. If one shall be an unworthy spirit and shall have left the bodily vehicle and be dwelling in spirit form but still earthbound because of lowly spiritual advancement and heavy spirit conditioning, that one then will roam about the earth disembodied, and there that one will be hardly subject at all to our ministrations, and our offers of help, even to our controlling, (although a large degree of control can usually be exercised, but in some cases it is even necessary to close hastily such a gathering as this because of, possibly, the influx of a very earthy one who is correspondingly powerful upon the earth). If that one were permitted to reincarnate just because he wished to escape from the unhappy circumstances in which he finds himself, it were not just, it were not reasonable and it would not help him or his spirit, for he must pass through the fires of his own thinking, he must arrive at a purification of himself and then he shall rise into a sphere which is more fitting for the spirit of man discarnate. But that he should return in order that he may continue, perhaps, upon his evil ways, that cannot be allowed.

I do not suppose that I can deal the theory a death blow, if only because there are instances, as I have already admitted or maintained, of voluntary, desirable reincarnation, and when one such shall appear to come before the notice of those who hold this theory as a gospel they will regard it as bolstering their theory 'in toto', which it does not do. But – a small point and yet a vital one – it does not matter how long in terms of the rotation of the earth, the universe of which you have knowledge has continued or shall continue, it is temporal; it is bounded and bounden by and in time, and spirit existence is *not* so bounded. Now, I will ask you to revolve the matter in your minds, bearing that most strongly in the forefront. Is it reasonable that the spirit, which is eternal – (eternal in both directions, if I may say so; it is eternal and ever-lasting, and I am aware that I am using terms which connote *time* to you but I wish you to dispel that thought from your minds, I do not want to introduce the idea of eternity as being an endless succession of years, it is not so) – you have been given the phrase "the ever-present now" which may or may not have meaning for you, but if you can endeavour to give it some meaning in order to avoid this suggestion of an eternity of years – then is it reasonable to suppose that spirit, which transcends time in such a manner, should be beholden to a time-burdened universe for its information, for its evolution, for its development, or is the reverse a more reasonable proposition? I will ask you to think it over.

We will pass on if you wish a few thousand million of your earth years and it may be that there will still be spirit incarnate upon the earth-plane in the form of man (of what nature, of what kind, I cannot envisage for I do not know) it may be so, but still they will be living in *time*, whereas spirit, from which they stem and of which they will be a part (just as you, my children, are a part) will still be then as it is now and as it was a thousand million of your years back in the past. Which then is the fundamental, which is the basic, which is quite obviously the starting point; which depends upon which? The question will resolve itself in your own mind, if you will turn it over.

Questioner. Going back hundreds of millions of years, before, as we are told, there was actually mankind upon the earth, is it possible to explain how and where the spirit-world was actually functioning then?

Abu. The spirit-world has always functioned, my son, but before there was mankind upon the earth there was not *individualised* spirit. Spirit was all pervading, all permeating and prior to what I suppose I may refer to as the creation of your universe, there was spirit and only spirit, and spirit was then – and this is the very process of creation – spirit was then apportioned off, as it were, for the purpose of manifesting, and ultimately (penultimately, perhaps I may say) to individualise in the form of the spirit of man, and so whilst spirit always was, the spirit world of which you now have knowledge, even the successive spirit-world of which you now have knowledge, had no factual existence, but of course, since all things are, they were even then, but not in form as at present.

Possibly there will be considerable physical changes, which may even be apparent to you now as commencing, but quite certainly there will be enormous changes in the mental world upon the earth-plane; the power of the mind of man, operated by his informing spirit, will increase and increase and increase, and I am prayerful, that such increase in the mental capacity, the mental powers of man, shall be directed by spiritual advancement rather than by spiritual regression. For man, as I have stated earlier, may rise to be God (for man potentially and fundamentally is God), but man can, and he so wish, depress himself spiritually into the semblance of a very devil if he shall so wish. I have no great fear upon the point myself. It is what you would describe as a long term view, do not take undue comfort from it! When you shall join hands with me, then together we may look and smile perhaps a little pityingly upon the earth's surface and we may have regard to what may then be going on, and you – like myself at the moment – will be untouched thereby, except by the compassion within your heart, which may stir you and may move you, as it has done me, to an endeavour to see if it is possible to shine the tiniest of candles into the gloom and the darkness which, I am thankful to say and to know, we have to some degree been able to dispel, and we are still engaged in dispelling it.

Questioner. Has there ever been individualisation elsewhere than on this earth?

Abu. Yes, indeed. I have referred to a number of universes of which necessarily my own knowledge is but indirect, and you will recall, I am sure, that we spoke of the tangents of the circles, or of spheres, and whether contact was made the one with the other, and it is from those realms that the information is derived – the information that there are other universes than yours in existence.

Questioner. I think the point was individualisation elsewhere than on earth.

Abu. Indeed there are individualisations, but other in nature than yours – than ours, I should say. But fundamentally, you will recall, there is but one spirit, it is all the same spirit, it is only the manifestation which differs, and so although the individualisation may and does take manifold forms, and the mental capacities will vary enormously, none the less the informing spirit behind all these experiments is the same, it has but one fount and that is him whom we know as God, the source of all life, of all light, of all warmth, and of all love, on no matter what universe. He is the source, and therein, if you can permit a concept so vast that it staggers me and must necessarily stagger you, if you can admit such a concept within your minds, it will be apparent to you how very parochial and how very foolish are sects upon the earth-plane who claim to have uniquely and exclusively the command and the control of such a one as I am endeavouring to picture God to be.

Questioner. Am I wrong in thinking that you said it was possible to reincarnate on one of the other spheres of existence and when I say that I mean not the spirit spheres, but material spheres.

Abu. The general answer, is no, because – (I must use the word time, unfortunately), by the time you shall have reached such a height as to contemplate a reincarnation (I will admit the word with the understanding of what you refer to) by the time you shall have reached such a height that you can consider reincarnating within a universe other than this of ours, the question will long since have ceased to have meaning, even for you, and so for practical politics it does not exist. In general terms, whilst your individuality and your personality continues, as it will do, as I have told you for a very long time (again this unfortunate word!) whilst that persists, you like myself, will be locked to the spirit spheres which surround this particular planet of this particular system which you know as the earth and the solar system. And there is ample space, and ample room for our development herein! We will consider our subsequent progress when we have outstripped all the possibilities at present lying before us.

Questioner. We are looking too far ahead.

Abu. Just a little, perhaps.

Questioner. I think it is very brave of any of you, to come back into our world to endeavour to bring teaching.

Abu. I find the words of my child sweet to my heart. I would assure you, my child, and all of my children that I and many others like me have but one regret at returning to be close to the earthplane, that regret being the very loss of potency of which I spoke this evening a little earlier. For we are, so many of us, vastly filled with enthusiasm, with the greatest of intentions, with the greatest of desire, and when we shall descend and descend into the ever heavier and darker and more gloomy conditions which it is necessary that we shall undertake, we find our hands more and more tied, more and more unable to do that which we so much long to do, and yet the longing and the yearning remains with us; it is only the potential which is withheld. But there is no doubt that our loving father knew what he was doing, it was not unkindly meant; for were we, even I Abu, able to bring the force, the power, the potency which is ours upon the sphere where we dwell, and to apply that in its full strength upon the earth-plane, the affairs of the earth-world would be conducted then by *us* and not by you, and that would not follow the intent, for the "horses" are yours, my children. I may be permitted, as I am permitted, as I am proud that I am permitted, to whisper in your ear, but you hold the reins, always you must hold the reins. I cannot, because I may not, endeavour to take them from your hands, and I have given you the more or less physical reason, for that. The desire is there, yes, indeed, to lift up my children that they dash not their feet against a stone, but that would be to deny the whole purpose of your life upon the earth-plane.

And so, with this little whisper which I am permitted, I will leave you now, and I can but say how happy it makes me, despite my degree of disappointment at not being able to do that which I would wish to do, to know that in the greatest thing of all, the knowledge of love and of its vital importance, in *that* my children have stepped a very considerable way with me, and for that I am proud and happy.

Chapter Twenty-Five

PRE-NATAL AWARENESS

Questioner. If a spirit, developed by earth experience, can enter into an as yet unborn body, in what sense does it follow the normal process of "becoming", in harmony with the physical "becoming"?

You have suggested that, in ordinary cases, there was no developed spirit which could select a physical envelope, but, if it can happen, then the argument against general reincarnation loses some of its force. There must, one supposes, be a 'pattern' in conforming to which each spirit fulfils its destiny and one can conceive of previous experience affecting that pattern whilst it appears to be necessary for each spirit to start 'ab initio', so to speak, and follow the normal process of "becoming".

Perhaps, in the special cases of reincarnation to which you refer, there is a pre-natal awareness of the path in front which is not possessed by the generality of spirit incarnations and yet that awareness may be lost – voluntarily lost – in the process of growth.

Will you comment on these ideas?

Abu. It would appear to me that you have largely answered your own question in that you suggest, towards the end of the question itself, having regard to the premise that the reincarnations of which I have spoken imply a developed and individualised spirit in the first instance, you then proceed to assume – and quite correctly – that the development of this particular, individualised spirit is held "in abeyance" during the process of becoming. And that is the short answer.

For, whilst I have, should I say denied (denied as within my own knowledge) the general rule of compulsory reincarnation for the spirits of all men, I have at the same time confessed to the possibility (again within my knowledge) of reincarnation in another physical vessel in specific instances. Your difficulty appears to arise from just the point which I made, namely, that in the first instance, in the ordinary course of events, there is no developed individualised spirit which could make a choice. Then you proceed to argue that, if a specific reincarnation is possible and does occur, in that instance there *is* an individualised and developed spirit which *can* choose and you then inquire:- Why does that development not allow itself to be seen from the very beginning? Is that the sense of your difficulty? Your actual phrase escapes me but, towards the end of the question . . .

Questioner. I will re-read that. 'Perhaps in the special cases to which you refer, there is a pre-natal awareness of the path in front which is not possessed by the generality of spirit incarnations and yet that awareness may be lost – voluntarily lost – in the process of growth'.

Abu. Thank you. Now, that is the point that I would take up. The pre-natal knowledge to which you refer is *not* lost. It is, to use the words which I have already employed, voluntarily and deliberately "held in abeyance"; it is suppressed whilst the physical vehicle is developing to a stature where it can

102

support the "prior intent" of the reincarnated spirit. Because, it would be pointless for the individualised spirit to endeavour to commence his or her mission whilst at a very tender age physically. Therefore the intent is held in abeyance for a period whilst the vessel does develop to the necessary degree. Does that introduce further difficulties?

Questioner. *It involves, of course, a process which you have not so far dealt with – a holding in abeyance. Your words were: "The spirit becomes as the man becomes".*

Abu. That was my phrase and you will appreciate that, if the spirit or the "portion" of spirit, itself is not already individualised as I have suggested, then it will become as the physical man becomes. But, granting that it is an already individualised spirit, it cannot enter into an existent, fully developed physical body but must, with patience, hold itself in restraint until the vehicle which it has chosen shall reach a suitable stage of growth.

Therefore, it is not necessary for that particular, individualised spirit to *begin* the process of becoming. That has already been done in a prior incarnation. Hence the necessity for restraint, for holding in abeyance, as I have said, the particular qualities which this spirit proposes to make use of and to exert upon the world of his fellow-men.

And, it must also be remembered that the physical body will not necessarily respond completely to the impact of the informing spirit in so far as what I must call 'cerebral' knowledge is concerned. In other words – and not to make greater difficulties yet – it is possible that the reincarnated spirit will be fully aware of the purposes of his reincarnation and yet the brain which he, the spirit, is informing and making use of will be unable to put this particular thing into a 'crystallised' form. But the driving force will be there, the urge will be there. The brain perhaps may be incapable of grasping fully the purpose, the intent, for all these things, but be *aware* none the less of the purpose.

I would not wish to trespass upon fields which are primarily religious for I know that many feet are tender on the matter and I prefer not to discuss them at great length, but I must refer you to your Jesus of Nazareth who himself, in that incarnation, was a reincarnated spirit and *was* aware of his purpose and his function and what he was trying to do. It is relatively rare for such a case to exist, but, even when the physical brain is not so aware as was his, even so the urge will be felt and will be responded to. Does that clear the ground at all?

You will appreciate, of course, that my remarks about the spirit becoming as the man becomes must be taken generally and not necessarily specifically. I do not mean that the spirit in some material way increases in stature as does the physical vehicle – of course I do not mean that. I cannot, and you will appreciate this, I cannot relate the stature of the spirit with the stature of the physical vessel which it will inhabit. But, since the physical vessel *has* to be developed, has to be evolved to the normal which is "man", then the informing spirit – to a degree blindly – will continue that process of so informing the vessel and so directing its evolution and its development. That process will continue, will go on, in exactly the same way whether it be what we must call a "new" spirit or whether it be a

103

reincarnation. So that the child – the body child – of the spirit which is to reincarnate will receive the same direction, the same evolution, the same development in terms of physical growth, from the informing spirit, as does the child body of a new spirit. It is the purpose, the function, which is held in abeyance for a time.

Questioner. It seems to me that, though time in a way may not matter, the time before such a spirit, developing in a child, comes to act, looks like a waste of time. Perhaps, before it can really act on the lines it is supposed to act, the need for it may have passed.

Abu. Put quite simply – the child is wishful that the "instrument shall play before it is completed". It cannot be. It is not a question of waste of time for, believe me my child, believe me, although I have said and others of us have said to you that over here one cannot 'waste time', that time has no real meaning, we are none the less fully conscious that for *you* time has considerable importance and that, therefore, our endeavours in your direction are in that sense timebound.

But, I have postulated a reincarnating spirit, with, perhaps, some great work that he wishes to carry out upon the earth-plane, and would you wish that spirit to commence that work at the bodily age of three years? That is all there is to say.

Questioner. But, if such a spirit came back to earth to try and help, could he not somehow set aside a spirit or overpower the existing spirit in someone and act through that person instead of waiting till the child grew up?

Abu. There are two misconceptions in what the child has said. In the first place, is she not aware that a vast amount of influence and inspiration is now and always has been poured down upon your earth-plane by the intermediary of spirit-mind in contact with spirit-mind incarnate? Inspiration, influencing yes; by far the greater part of the work of the spirit world is done in such a manner. There you have the individualised and developed spirit endeavouring to work as directly as possible without this business of reincarnating – which is what you ask for.

Your second point – which I *must* take up – was a suggestion (I do not know if you meant to use the word in this sense) that the developed spirit should 'overpower' an existing, bodily vehicle, inhabited by the spirit of another person, and make use of that vehicle for his purposes. That my child, would be *possession*. It is done by *lower* orders, by the unworthy ones, but it is not rightful, for the 'portion' of spirit which is in process of becoming, of individualising, has a right and is the only spirit which has any right, to the physical vessel which he is using. It is only what I must again call the lower type – the lower order – of spirit (I do not care to speak of it) which would venture so to 'overpower' – granted that the link between the spirit and the body is so weak that the overpowering is possible – it would never be done by a spirit with a good intent except with the express permission and invitatation of the person concerned – as witness this present moment.

Matters are, of course, at times involved. There is always the difficulty of the point of view, for a thing, a 'happening', may look very different indeed when viewed from perhaps opposing angles and that, unfortunately, is not infrequently our case. You will look upon happenings upon the earth-plane and find it difficult to reconcile them with a loving Father. I, on the other hand, can view the same happenings and, whilst feeling an extreme compassion within my own heart, since man must suffer therefore, I do not find them incompatible with this love and I cannot explain to you in your own terminology what I can feel about the matter. It is a question of the point of view and that is why I have been – have permitted myself to be – "dogmatic" on the point, instead of, as would have been reasonable, demonstrating to you the love of God of which I have spoken so often. I have merely insisted upon it. For, it is the yardstick, my son, by which all things must and should be judged and, if you will question your yardstick, it will cease to have great value for you.

Regrettably, I must continue to be dogmatic on the point. I do not wish you to think that I am saying – what is the phrase? "God is in His Heaven and all is well with the world" – (there is a phrase to that effect) – because, all is *not* well with the world and no one, I think, is more conscious of that than I myself – for I have other contacts than this.

But, none the less, through it all does run the golden thread, the thread of the love of God – and here again I dogmatise! What else can I do? What else can I do? Things are as they are and they must and can and will be modified, without any doubt at all, until all men shall see, in their daily lives, in their impact with their fellow-men, in their contact with the spirit world – shall *see* the love of God. It shall be patent and manifest. Such, unhappily is not yet entirely the case. You have a glimpse here and there. I have commented on this in an earlier talk – that there are the things of beauty, of love, of warmth, which are the reflections of the love of God – you have these glimpses – yes.

Questioner. 'Glimpses' we do have and I think our relationship with you has given us the brightest glimpse of all.

Abu. I am happy that it should be so for, were it not so, then my mission were wasted. But I know that you must, all of you, so often in your daily lives, see things, see happenings and instances, which do not appear to be compatible. There again Abu dogmatises and says: "My children, it is in the point of view".

These things which are wrong *are* wrong for men. Yes, they are and many of them – most of them, indeed – are man-made obstacles. When man shall grow in spiritual stature, when he shall see the glimpses and gleams of light which even now assail his eyes and insist upon the love of God, when he shall see that these things are in very truth the divine light which he should seek and to which he should turn his eyes and he then begins so to do – then, my son, will these unhappy things, one by one, be sloughed off from the life of man.

For, man should be happy – I have said it before and I will continue to say it. In the spirit world of evolved spirits (I do not speak of those whom I have called unworthy for they – poor souls – are in no better plight than they were when incarnate) but in the spirit world of evolved and developed spirits, up and up and up the divine "ladder" of which we have spoken, there *is* happiness – happiness increasing and increasing – and there should be happiness upon the earth-plane. There *will* be happiness upon the earth-plane, but man must find that happiness by opening his eyes. In the meantime, whilst things *do* occur which offend, which bring sorrow and grief and trouble to the heart and the soul of man – whilst these things must continue upon the earth-plane, I can only say – the golden light *does* lie behind it all and one day men will see it clearly.

Here, I insist upon apologising, for I dogmatise and I would that I did not have to do so! But, it is in the point of view – my angle differs from yours.

So, I am happy that my children have taken – not my teachings alone – but these teachings, from whatever source, to their hearts and that you are able to smile in the face of all the adversities which assail you and to know that what we speak is true: that the Love of God *does* shine forth and *will* shine forth. The lot of man upon the earth *will* improve – his spirituality, his spiritual stature – and with them, his happiness.

Bless you, my children.

Chapter Twenty-Six

RETURN TO REINCARNATION

Questioner. In a book I have been reading it is stated that it is impossible for any soul to understand reincarnation until the celestial sphere is reached (whatever that term may be taken to mean). The suggestion is that every soul has, at some time, left those celestial spheres for a sojourn upon earth or some other planet, with no memory of its identity upon that sphere until it has been through a life upon the earth and returns to that sphere, when all previous lives and incarnations are made known to it. It is then suggested that, if the soul discovers that the work it has set out to do has not yet been completed, the 'facet' – that is the term used – of that soul can come back to the earth, or some other planet, and finish its work. Does that mean that it is part of a group soul which comes back and not a particular individual? Is that within your knowledge?

Abu. I have already endeavoured to explain that I have no knowledge of any universal reincarnation. The voluntary, deliberate and intentional reincarnations for an express, specific and permitted purpose, of which I have had knowledge, have been from planes or spheres considerably below those which you are now terming the 'celestial', for it has been the express intent of the thinking mind of the spirit who has wished to reincarnate upon the earth's surface that he should do so and, if he shall be merely one facet of some larger group soul, he as an individual surely would hardly have competency in the matter, and therein lies, as I see it, a difficulty.

We are speaking largely of transcendental things; we are speaking of 'celestial spheres' which, by my own admission are necessarily removed beyond personality – beyond human personality – and therefore I cannot, with any intelligence, discuss what may occur in regions where human personality does not hold sway, for I do not know, and I venture to submit that neither does anyone else who is a human person. When you shall have transcended personality you will no longer be able to convey to a limited *person* anything of which you are aware, because you are no longer a person to *be* aware in a personal manner, and of that I cannot speak, for I have no knowledge. It may be that it is so in the celestial spheres of which you speak: it may be – I do not know. I submit that it cannot be known. But if it shall be so and a part or section of mankind shall be but a recurring reincarnation of facets, as it were, in the form of individuals, I will submit to you (this is purely reason, not an expression of opinion, for I do not know what may or may not transpire at such a rarified altitude) that the incarnation which will spend but a few short years upon your little ball in space and is sent down or voluntarily comes down – I do not know which is preferred – from a region which embraces the whole of your world and touches upon a vastly greater universe than you could even at present conceive (this by your own showing and that of your teacher) . . . is it reasonable, my son?

The suggestion would appear to me to be parallel with this one – which I think you will agree is as ridiculous as it sounds. There shall be a successful business man, perhaps, in your world – successful in a business sense in the eyes of your world since he can make lots of money and is in all those senses a very successful man, but he has forgotten some trivial item of his arithmetic – he can no longer extract a square root – and so he must go and spend another two or three years at a child's school when he has achieved the *ability* to succeed (as your world regards success) and having arrived at such an eminence, he must now return to the kindergarten, which he left forty or fifty years ago because, forsooth, he can no longer extract a square root. But he has extracted the virtue from the square root by having *succeeded*; he does not need the square root any more. And, when a soul, when a spirit, when a man – for we are men – shall have arrived at such an eminence as the celestial spheres – or considerably lower – it is little short of childish to suggest that he must return and begin again to learn to 'tie his bootlaces'! I will have none of it. I am sorry if I offend at all for I have no intention of offending.

Questioner. There is no offence. I have been reading those particular teachings and they puzzled me.

Abu. I am happy to speak with you upon the matter. With regard to the transcendental or celestial spheres (I will adopt your term) I can know nothing of them because I am personal; I shall remain personal for a very long time yet, and transcendental spheres cannot *be* personal, for they transcend personality, and therefore I can know nothing of them and I submit that neither can any *other* person.

Questioner. But you do imply that one can reach a transcendental stage?

Abu. It is implied without a doubt: most certainly it is implied and is implicit in my teaching that we, spirit man or woman, will all ultimately, at an infinity of distance and of time which we cannot at all conceive – because again the concept is transcendental – will 'arrive', if one may use the term, at the Godhead – at the state of *being* God; but it would be ridiculous for me to say that, when we shall get there, we shall sit down and have 'steak and chips' for our dinner! For that is what your proposition is asking me to admit and I cannot do it.

I know from personal experience that the spirit of man, once incarnate, will and does reach to what we have agreed to call the Christ sphere and for me that is the limit. I cannot conceive of going beyond; whether it is that the spheres thereupon become celestial and therefore transcendental and therefore impersonal and therefore non-human, I do not know. I cannot know: I have not ventured into such spheres and it is quite obvious to you, by the very terms of reference to such spheres, that I could not enter into such spheres; and neither could you and remain a limited person. You must, if it be so, be absorbed into something yet vaster, yet greater, and that may *be*. I agree, it is implied: it may be, but I cannot speak from personal knowledge for I do not know.

Questioner. Would that be what is termed the 'second death'?

Abu. It could be that which is refered to as the second death, for indeed in terms of human personality it would succeed in being something more nearly of the nature of true death than is the physical death which you know upon earth, for by the terms of reference – and again I speak without personal knowledge – the personality will be expunged and extinguished in such an act, and that of course is death to the *person*. To the spirit it may be continuing life, for the spirit lived before the person was a person, as I have so often told you, and it is quite certain that the spirit will continue to live after the person has ceased to be a person; but we need not concern ourselves with that for we shall not be there to concern ourselves. It is going rather further than we are in the habit of going, for we have a great deal of *matter* before us which we can usefully discuss before we need to venture into transcendental fields such as that.

I have – of course I have – to give you a little warning: that if a teacher – I do not mind who he is – shall claim that he is aware (in a human sense, in the sense of knowing, as you know and I know) of being at one with the Godhead and of knowing what goes on in such transcendental regions, he is a little suspect, for he cannot have experienced that which is beyond human experience; it is impossible. Man, as I have claimed, is part of God but he is not the whole of God, and God is not man. God subsists in his creations and God transcends his creations, and man – the creation of mankind upon earth, his subsequent dwelling upon innumerable spirit spheres until he shall reach this transcendental stage – is a part of the God 'experiment' of individualisation which, for inscrutable purposes, is adding something to the quality of the spirit which was, is, and will be God. It may be that individuality or personality at some stage – such as the celestial spheres – may necessarily be expunged, but if it is so, no *person* can tell you of what occurs thereafter for there is no *person*, there is no one, to come back and therefore you must treat as a little suspect any description of spheres in which it is stated that human personality has ceased to exist, for if that is indeed so, how can human personality know of it?

Assumption, yes; theorizing, yes; hypothecating, yes; by all means let us do these things if they will be of any use to us. Personally, I am limited: I have never claimed to be other than limited, and I know that the spirit of man and woman remains human, remains as personal as upon the earth, up to what I have called the Christ sphere. I have not travelled higher than that; I have no wish to do so and I do not know if it is possible to do so. From that point, where the personality is still remaining but the spiritual development and evolution of the individual has been brought to its highest possible pitch – from that point to God, is certainly a vast step and I cannot begin to place one foot in that direction, but it is still God, it is all God, for there is nothing but God.

You will have much to think upon and to talk about. I regret extremely if I shall have been less able than usual to give you information, but you have, by implication, asked for information where none could – by the very terms of reference – be available. In the meantime I would ask that you will not allow yourselves to feel belittled or in any way downcast by thinking of your present stature in comparison with these godlike beings of whom we have been speaking, for they were as you are and you shall be as they are.

We have our little duties to do: to love our fellows, to love one another, to spread the knowledge that this spirit which is God is the spirit which is Love, and that only by expressing, through teaching and through showing forth, that love on each and every plane of existence, are we doing that which the spirit of ourselves – your own spirits – knows is rightful and the thing that it would wish to do. More than that cannot be asked.

Chapter Twenty-Seven

THE "GOLDEN AGE"

Abu. As I have told you in the past when I originally referred to this 'Golden Age', it occurred not upon this planet of yours at all. It occurred, I then said, upon a sphere – always a 'sphere'! – not now comprised in your Cosmos at all and no real recollection in terms of remembered happenings remains of that Golden Age in the minds of men who have incarnated upon the earth's surface.

Because – and here I tread upon the mystical and here is where you will begin to raise objection, I am to tell you that the Golden Age of which I speak was a form of earlier experimentation in the manifestation of Spirit in form – do you follow my words? As I have already made clear, the opinions which I express are my opinions, I would not wish that they were held to be authoritative; I put them forward as the opinions of a mind which has had opportunity of seeking and of learning to some degree and I put them forward as reasonable and logical to a degree for the consideration of the reason of my children, but, if you please, not authoritative. And so that is why I was not *averse* to discussing the matter, but a little afraid that you would find the 'logic' of which I speak has been perhaps a little jettisoned when I bring forward the proposition which I am now offering you.

But, as you know, I hold the view that man upon the earth – and I wish to include in the term 'man' the remainder of the animal creation, possibly some of what you know as the vegetable kingdom – creation, then, the appearance of life upon the earth – is the undifferentiated spirit in manifestation. I have also said in the past and I repeat it here and now that this manifestation is far from being the only one which is contemporary with your own. I have already touched upon this point – that there are other manifestations of spirit in form elsewhere than upon your earth – and the 'Golden Age' of which I have spoken was an earlier manifestation – an earlier attempt shall I say – at a satisfactorily evolved manifestation of spirit in form and shape.

I will refer yet again to your 'book', to the allegorical picture which is there given you of the creation of your world, in which the creation of the animal kingdom and finally of man is dealt with in terms that would indicate that it was then and there taking place upon the surface of the earth. But, this story is merely an allegory and it refers not to the manifestation of spirit in form upon the earth but to the Golden Age, the very Golden Age of which I speak. For the story of your forefather and your foremother (my words are probably incorrect) but that story of their time of blessedness in a certain garden as it is described occurred during the Golden Age and elsewhere than upon your earth. And the story, as an allegory, must be regarded as a partial and imperfect recollection of circumstances which existed in the dim and distant past – given that Time then existed, which it did not – and in another place which does not now exist at all!

For the experiment was found to be ineffective – I cannot say a failure, but ineffective. Elsewhere than in this Cosmos of yours, this closed universe of yours which your scientists are beginning to learn so much about, elsewhere than within this soap-bubble of your universe, there was created (I must use words such as that otherwise my speech would become laborious, you understand) there was created, then, a sphere not entirely dissimilar to your own but not precisely the same, and upon this sphere was commenced an early attempt (it was not the first, but an early attempt) at the manifestation of spirit into form. And that is, or was, the Golden Age of which I have spoken wherein the Spirit essence took unto itself form; not precisely in the shape of man and woman as you know yourselves but, again, very similar indeed.

But, they were, as your story of Adam and Eve will tell you, in a condition of perfect blessedness. There was, in a word, no 'evil', no possibility of evil, in this particular manifestation of creation. It pertained quite largely to the nature of what you know as the 'spirit world', that is to say the next step beyond your earth-plane, but it was more – not more perfect but less imperfect – than that spirit world itself is because, in the spirit world as you know it there is still the knowledge of and the recollection of 'evil', and in the Golden Age evil had not then existed at all.

One of your poets has drawn a picture which, maybe, will come to your mind of a proud spirit dwelling in Heaven and being cast therefrom. You will appreciate to what I refer. That again is an allegory and it refers to yet another 'fall of man' in that the spirit (spirits in fact, of course) dwelling in a state of complete blessedness, without any evil at all, was required (and here again come the 'inscrutable reasons' into which I cannot enter for I do not know them) the spirit was required to know of evil and that could not be achieved upon the sphere to which I have referred and so the spirit essence which had become to some degree individualised (although not individualised as is man and woman upon the earth-plane but to some degree individualised) was as it were 'remixed' again and there commenced subsequently the new experiment of which you are part and in which you are taking part.

During its sojourn upon the earth-plane, as you are all too well and too sadly aware, the spirit which has required itself to undergo these experiences has contacted evil and will continue to contact evil for a long, long while to come. Why this should be, I beg that you will not ask me for I do not know, but that is the picture which I must give you. And there are dim, very dim, shall I say 'race memories' – it is not a happy phrase for it is not sufficiently all embracing, for the race memory to which I refer should embrace far more than a race, it should embrace the whole human race – but there are dim 'race memories' of that time which persist and which come occasionally to light in the writings of certain inspired ones upon your world and make themselves seen, to be misinterpreted as so many things are misinterpreted by the conscious, thinking mind of man.

That, however, is the 'Golden Age' to which I have referred when man, whilst not yet man, was none the less crystallising and differentiating his spirit from the formless sea of Spirit-ether of which I have spoken, but in conditions where no evil could exist or could even be *thought*, and that of course *would* appear to you a 'Golden Age'. So it is to that stage of spirit existence that I ventured to refer. And now I await a torrent of questions and objections!

Questioner. You referred to the allegorical story of Adam and Eve in the bible as picturing the Golden Age; it would appear that whoever was inspired in the writing of our Bible had some conscious or unconscious recollection of this Golden Age which caused him to introduce it into the beginning of that bible. I presume that we must read into that allegory that the Golden Age finished upon the entrance of evil.

Abu. The Golden Age was concluded but not upon the entrance of evil for no evil entered therein, but upon the reconstituting of the spirit matter which had begun to individualise and the commencement of the new experiment which has resulted in man as he now is upon the earth-plane, wherein was already evil in potential of course. And so your story of Adam and Eve, whilst being 'factual', if I may use the word, is not factual upon the earth-plane. And therein lies a difficulty which is sometimes felt by certain of your thinkers in that they will wish to deny that man has ever suffered a 'fall'. On the contrary, they say, man has begun from lowly beginnings and has slowly, and is continuing slowly, to fight his way upwards. That is perfectly true upon the earth-plane, but the thinkers do not, because they cannot, have regard to the commencement of existence – of potential human existence – otherwise than upon the earth-plane. And therein lies the 'fall'; It was not a fall in the sense that man gave himself over to evil where he had no need so to do – quite the contrary. In the Golden Age, upon this other sphere of which I speak, the spirit which ultimately was to become man was not subject to evil and therefore could not develop in the same manner and to the same degree as he is compelled to develop upon your earth through the hard knocks which he must undergo – 'slings and arrows' is, I believe, the phrase – and so there was a 'fall' in that the condition of living with and by and in touch with evil is a 'lower' order of existence perhaps than that which I have referred to as the Golden Age or than that which you shall subsequently enter into. There was a fall but it was not a fall due to a *fault* of man: it was not the doing of man at all. It was the commencement of yet another experiment.

Questioner. You have taught us to regard evil as the absence of light or of 'good', rather than as a positive thing. I cannot as yet, form any picture of a state in which man, or anything resembling man, being of necessity an imperfect creature and therefore necessarily imperfectly illuminated by the light of Spirit and consequently having what we are forced to call 'evil' inherent in him – I cannot, I say, picture man existing in any recognisable way with nothing of that evil in him – with only light, only good, as you have pictured him.

Abu. Your fallacy is in the assumption that evil is implicit in man. Evil is not implicit in spirit: spirit is not evil.

Questioner. It is the absence of light, the imperfect illumination of things by Spirit, which I have been thinking of as 'evil'. Perhaps I am wrong in so doing.

Abu. I think I take your difficulty, but, perhaps unfortunately, it is no difficulty to *me*! I will ask you to cast your mind forward to what you regard as the 'spirit-world', to the next phase of existence, wherein I have claimed that there *exists* no evil but there is *recollection* of evil. There exists no evil for a number of reasons but, for one reason – to invent a simple case – if one upon your earth-plane shall desire to injure another, there is nothing to prevent him other than the fear of repercussions, the fear of your law or something of the kind – he is not prevented otherwise. But upon the next plane of existence, if you shall feel harshly against a fellow-being it is not possible for you to do that fellow-being an injury for you are mutually repellent the one to the other and you cannot approach thereto. That particular phase of evil is therefore not in existence, but still you will have recollection of your earthly existence during which time it was possible to exert an evil influence.

I must refer you (it is perhaps apposite as it touches upon a germane matter) to the words of our very dear mutual friend who keeps the door, who was referring a little earlier this evening to bodily ailments and pains. You see, within his mind is a recollection of the fact that once, for him, bodily pain did exist. He is reminded by contact with you that for you bodily pain still exists: for him it does not, therefore he cannot suffer. Correspondingly, with regard to the question of doing evil, exactly the same position applies. If a person – the spirit of a person – should wish to do evil, he will find himself unable to do so in that sphere, upon that particular plane. If his mind be so set upon the practising of evil that he actively wishes to practise something which he himself will appreciate as being a wrong and unworthy act, then he will translate himself to a sphere where he can, potentially, perform this evil and have evil performed upon him. Does that help at all?

Questioner. The only thing that still puzzles me is that, in referring to this Golden Age, you speak of man, or some being recognisable as man. But that is not a spirit world pure and simple; it is a material world I suppose. You did say it was a manifestation in form and so must be thought of as a 'material' world.

Abu. It is what you would know as a material world.

Questioner. So that when you speak of the next phase of existence and the absence of evil there I cannot apply this to any variety of 'manifestation in form' or, in other words, a 'material' world.

Abu. I knew you would have a great difficulty in comprehending this whole theme because I have necessarily had to step beyond the bounds of Time and of Space and also, as I forewarned you, the bounds of logic. I must ask for an imaginative effort on your part.

You are aware of your world as at present constituted as containing a great deal of active evil – to use that word – and a very great deal more of evil which is passive and waiting but opportunity to show itself forth. Is that not so? But you are equally aware of men upon your earth's surface whom you would describe perhaps as 'saint-like'. If you will now imagine (and it will take a great deal of imagining, I am aware) if you will imagine the whole population of the world being as saint-like as and more saint-like than the most saintly man of whom you can think at present, you will gain some appreciation of the circumstances which existed upon this other sphere. It is an impossibility for you to imagine this but you can perhaps imaginatively conceive or at least concede the notion.

Questioner. I fancy the thing we cannot imagine is that such an existence as that could be a 'failure' or anything approaching it. Of course the thing we cannot understand and which you say you cannot explain is why evil was deemed to be necessary in the evolution of man.

Abu. I can offer you an analogy. I am, as you are aware, quite fond of analogies but often they must fail of their purpose and perhaps this one will fail similarly.

If you upon your earth-plane were wishful to construct something – I do not know of what nature – but to construct something from some of the more intractable material of your world, and you succeeded in constructing this something but it was not to your liking in that it was perhaps not as smooth or smoothly finished as you would wish it to be, you would take it to – what is your term, a whetstone? – a something which shall brutally grind away irregularities and finally succeed in producing the highly polished surface which you had originally intended and desired but which could not have been achieved without that brutal process. And the unhappy atoms comprising this intractable material, finding themselves in the position in which you as human beings find yourselves, will say: "We are here, we comprise and make up a something and we cannot conceive why our noses must be pressed to the grindstone thus". But the you who is making the something is fully aware that this brutal process is essential in order to produce the polish. It is but an analogy and I cannot give you *reasons* for I do not know the reasons, I merely know that they exist. The contact with what you know as evil upon your earth-plane, with all the possibilities of doing harm as well as good to your fellowmen is necessary, and further than that I cannot go.

Questioner. But it is part of the all-embracing love you have spoken of?

Abu. My sister, yes; for my son whom I had imagined as making this something, is grinding it away most tenderly and with the utmost love in his heart, but it would be difficult to persuade the individual molecules of the material that that was so.

Chapter Twenty-Eight

REFLECTIONS ON THE "GOLDEN AGE"

Questioner. You have stated that you have no knowledge of compulsory reincarnation as a general principle. From your talk on the Golden Age we inferred that this age was not a complete success because an individualised spirit gained no experience of evil and that our present earth-life was evolved to give this experience. Now, many spirits fail apparently to gain this experience for various reasons, e.g. 1. Death in childhood. 2. Passage through earth-life as an imbecile. 3. A sheltered earth-life which for various reasons gave no contact with the harsher experiences of life. Surely these spirits will have no memory of evil in the next phase of life and may feel it necessary to reincarnate. That is the first part of my question.

Abu. I thank you. It is a little alarming to realise that there will be a second part!

Now, I cannot enumerate all your categories but I will refer to one only: namely that of the person who passes from your earth-plane shortly after his or her birth thereupon, in early childhood as it were. That one, as you rightly suggest, will have had no experience of evil. The other categories, despite the suggestion implicit in your question, will none the less have made contact with what I must call evil, if only through contact with other human beings during the spell of their time on earth, and so knowledge of evil will come within their ken. I would not suggest and I would not wish you to think that I suggest, that there is any least necessity for each and every incarnating spirit to undergo personally all possible experiences of evil – that were a patent impossibility. But the *knowledge* of evil must necessarily come to you if you shall live upon your earth-plane for a sufficiently long time – a sufficient number of your years – to be able to appreciate the fact of evil, and that contact with evil is sufficient. Sufficient, that is to say, to enable the spirit of the person in question, when departing from your earth-plane and appearing upon the next phase of existence, to enable that person to understand and to appreciate what he or she (for sex continues in the next phase of life) is being shown, or has indicated to his spirit, in picture, in parable, in recital, wherein the notion of evil shall require to be introduced. That is sufficient, for, as I must repeat, it is quite evidently not necessary for each incarnating soul to undergo each and every experience possible of the good life – it cannot be.

But, you will recall that these matters of which we speak and to which we refer loosely at the moment as 'good' and 'evil' are spiritual attributes, and it is not necessary that each one of you shall come up against a given set of circumstances in order that you shall learn, as if at school, a certain lesson from that set of circumstances. That is the suggestion which underlies, generally speaking, the theory of compulsory universal reincarnation. But it is so palpable an absurdity, that you should have little difficulty, I think, in dismissing the validity of reincarnation so offered to you as being necessary for that reason, for it cannot be and, as I say, the absurdity will be palpable to you. But each and every person who lives for a reasonable period upon the earth will most certainly come into contact with – that is to say gain an appreciation of the *fact* of evil and that in itself suffices.

For the Golden Age of which I spoke held no evil, held no *concept* of evil. It was not that man, as man is upon the earth today, lived upon another planet just as man lives today upon this planet of yours, except that he lived a goodly and godly life and *avoided* evil. There *was* no evil: evil did not exist, it was not possible. That is why, to use your own words, the experiment was virtually a failure. Because (I have used this metaphor in the past) the 'edges' were not rounded off the life. It was not possible for the life to be 'smoothed off' as it should be and as it can be, following upon an earthly experience – an earthly evolution. But by far the greater lessons of the spirit in these respects will be learned upon the spirit-plane succeeding to your earth-plane, not upon the earth-plane itself. In other words, the earth-plane is a 'surface' (I do not like the word but I cannot find a better) a surface of experience, and the life in the next phase – the spirit world as it is known to you – is a 'surface' of learning where the contacts which are made during the earth experience will be assimilated into the spirit-stuff of which the spirit body and the spiritual nature of the individual is composed. Does that help at all or do I introduce further difficulties?

Questioner. I cannot as yet see how an imbecile can assimilate evil if he is unable to understand anything, unable even to read, for instance, of evil.

Abu. You are closing your eyes to a great deal to which they should be open. For the imbecile, in your terms, cannot read; he may be deaf and dumb, he may be blind; he may go through life as a deaf, dumb and blind imbecile and therefore to all seeming remote from contact with your world, but it still is not so. For there is the greater mind – what we have agreed without further argument to call the 'subconscious'. It is a greater part of the mind than what you know as the activating, conscious part of the mind, and that subconscious, I am maintaining, the greater portion of the mind even of the deaf, dumb and blind imbecile, is in fact making a contact, all unknown to his compeers, with the earth-world and its circumstances which shall suffice him as *experience*. Because (always recall) I speak of spiritual experiences and not of physical ones, and it shall suffice him when he shall awaken no longer blind, or deaf or dumb and certainly no longer imbecile, upon the spirit-plane of life.

Now, as to the children. Numbers without a doubt of tiny children live a very short earth-life – virtually no earth-life at all – and they are unable to undergo experiences and to achieve anything very much in the way either of good or of evil. Then these children, upon their transition, will be taken to a 'place' (I must use your spatial terms) where they can, as it were, grow up mentally and spiritually, as I believe you have been told, and such children will be brought again into touch with parents remaining upon the earth-plane or with parents departed from the earth-plane into the spirit world, in order that a family, for example, may be united – always given that the link of love exists, did exist and continues to exist. For, again as I have said, the blood tie is no tie at all; it is the link of love which matters and an unwanted child which was never loved will make no further contact with its parents, simply because they were not parents in

116

the spiritual sense but only in the physical, which does not matter. Then these children will grow up to an adult stature upon the spirit-plane of life, short of earth experience and they will advance and they will progress up and up through the spirit spheres just as the adult dweller upon earth will do.

But, as you will complain, this hypothetical child is still short of earth experience and therefore has not the same compass within its reach as is the case with the adult who has achieved, through experience, the knowledge of evil and the assimilation of spiritual lessons to be learned therefrom. That child – some of those children – *may* reincarnate; it is permitted. I have made that point in the past and I make the point again. I have claimed that compulsory reincarnation, universal compulsory reincarnation is not the fact, within my knowledge, but that voluntary reincarnation for a purpose is permitted – 'permitted' is perhaps hardly the word. For a reincarnation is potentially possible to any spirit since, when the vehicle is to be produced upon your earth-plane, that vehicle will be informed by spirit and whether it be spirit not previously incarnate or spirit which has already incarnated is not material. There is no 'squabbling for first place', you understand, and the child of whom I have spoken may, during his passage through spheres of spirit existence, become aware of the fact that he or she (whilst sex persists) has failed to undergo certain experiences which might have been undergone.

If thereupon, this soul, this spirit, shall decide that, for his own betterment, his own advancement, or for the advancement and preferment of others, a reincarnation would be desirable, then such will be permitted and so the child who failed to gain an earth experience at the first attempt will be given an opportunity to undergo such experience upon a second attempt, *if* so desired.

Questioner. But it is not necessary?

Abu. It is not necessary, my sister, and here as in the case of my little talk upon the Golden Age – I fear that I shall have to leave you behind a little. Because the reincarnation to which I refer takes place, not from the spirit life of which you have direct knowledge, but from a phase or plane in the spheres at which the spirit life arising (I am choosing my words with care) the spirit life arising from your planet begins to blend with spirit life arising from (I should not say 'arising from', it is not a correct word but I must leave it at that) spirit life then, arising from elsewhere than your world – and therefore the reincarnation to which I refer could conceivably take place not upon your earth but elsewhere in order that experience may be gained.

But the point at which I am with difficulty arriving and which you will not find greatly to your taste is this: that I have in the past, had occasion to displace man a little from his pedestal and to force home, a little unkindly, the fact that man is not the greatest of the spirit experiments. He is just *one* of a number of such experiments and therefore from the point of view of pure spirit, incarnation upon the earth-plane as man is *not* necessary, since the spiritual results which are to be achieved – which must be achieved – can be achieved by other means than that. In other words, *your* experiment is not a unique one. And so I feel I have left you a little behind for I appreciate that it must be very difficult indeed for you to get a realisation of the fact that, vast as is the scheme of things which I have had occasion to put before you, commencing with your earth-plane and proceeding up and up through the spheres, it is but one narrow corridor of a much, much vaster whole.

And so I could not – I could not – accede to any suggestion that an incarnation upon the earth was essential for the full development of spirit – with, if I may be allowed to say so, a capital S. If the child, the spirit – that is to say the portion of spirit – which should have become a man, upon reaching a spiritual status such as I have described, shall decide that an incarnation upon the earth-plane is desirable for its specific purpose, then that reincarnation will be permitted. But it may not do so and it will not suffer thereby.

Questioner. Is there no difference in the 'portion' of spirit which comes here for the first time or the second time ?

Abu. Except in terms of experience which has already been undergone, there is no difference. In essence the spirit is as it has always been. For I have claimed that Spirit is all-pervading and it is 'homogeneous', if I may use that word, and it shall have meaning for you. There is no difference in the spirit essence; but, to use a homely simile perhaps, if the spirit which is to be newly incarnated for the first time upon the earth-plane shall be regarded as 'white', perhaps the reincarnating spirit may be regarded as 'pink' or whatever colour its previous experience may have left upon the spirit.

Questioner. But it was previously individualised, wasn't it?

Abu. Prior individualisation upon the earth-plane, yes. But, if spirit shall come from another sphere completely (when I say 'sphere' I mean elsewhere than the series of classes which rise from your earth-plane) – elsewhere than that – if the spirit shall decide to incarnate upon the earth, following upon a set of experiences upon another sphere entirely, then that spirit, from the earth point of view, will appear as a new spirit because it has no previous earth experience. But the point is not very material – except to the incarnating spirit.

Questioner. In voluntary reincarnation, a second individuality is gained through a second earth experience. How are the two merged when again passing to spirit? The spirit has evolved through so many spheres that any individuality gained in its first earth experience may have been lost completely (though that is not a very good way of putting it) and reincarnation would not affect its individuality again. I don't feel satisfied with my question but am I right in this?

Abu. Reasonably you are right, but you castigate yourself unduly for your subsidiary question has a degree of interest. Actually nothing is *lost* – nothing at all is lost, but an effect is made upon the spirit. The spirit, to use another homely, earthly term, is moulded, shall we say, by the experiences which it has undergone during its incarnation and so the effects of those experiences remains whilst the experiences themselves being, as I have already said, of a temporal and evanescent nature, have indeed been lost, for they never *were* of importance or value, but merely their effect and that effect does remain.

But you are confusing the terms individuality and personality. The individual and his individuality persists, as again I have claimed, persists for a time which I cannot describe – certainly far, far beyond any thing that I myself have yet reached. And still and yet again there are individualities which are evolving elsewhere than in this one particular 'school' and we shall meet at some greater eminence, at some future 'date' – if you will permit that word – and we shall all be individuals. But, particularly in the case of successive reincarnations, either upon the earth or elsewhere, there will have been, during the period of existence (I cannot say the 'lifetime' – the period of existence) of that particular, individual spirit, a number of personalities, the *effect* of which will be made upon the individual, but the details of which will be sloughed off as of no importance.

For consider: when you yourself shall perform the act of death and shall pass into the next stage of existence – the spirit-life to you – you do not think that your experiences will cease? On the contrary, your experiences will only then truly *begin* and therefore you will build for yourself a 'personality'. It will not be identical with the one which you now have, because the impacts from without will differ, but the individual is above personality and that personality – the spirit-world personality – will add to the stature of the individual, will mould and will smooth the individual spirit. And that process will continue so that, by the time you shall arrive at a stage where you may decide for yourself whether you wish to reincarnate, either upon the earth or elsewhere or not at all, you will have the results of a very large number of personalities combined in your ever-present individuality.

Questioner. The 'effects' you speak of might be visible, even to us I suppose? Some people do seem to be different and to be naturally more knowledgeable in eternal things.

Abu. Yes, but it is a little difficult for me to speak upon the point because it would require a very close contact with the people of your earth-plane – a contact which I am not now able to make – and when I was upon the earth-plane and was able to make such contacts, of course these things meant much less to me than they do at present, and therefore I cannot answer your question succinctly and precisely. I will merely refer to the words which have been used by a mutual friend at the doorway. I believe he used the phrase: "You can see it on their faces, both those coming down from above and those coming up from below" – (to use those words) – and so your question is justified. These effects could be and frequently are observable, even by contemporaries such as yourself.

Questioner. There's just one other point. As you know, some apparently very evolved spirits do quite emphatically teach 'compulsory reincarnation'. Is it possible that they may really mean, not reincarnation in this sphere of life but that they are really meaning reincarnation somewhere else? Some individuals are very emphatic on this point of compulsory reincarnation.

2nd Questioner. If that is what they mean I think they should not use the word 'carnate' which implies inhabiting human flesh.

Abu. I thank you; it is the point that I was about to make, that, in that event, the word is poorly chosen. But you tell me that a number of highly evolved (from your point of view) spirits teach 'compulsory reincarnation'. I should be happy if you would kindly enquire into the suggestion and I will submit to you that you will find that the bulk of the teachings which emanate from a spirit teacher such as myself, who is named and as it were individualised among you, the bulk of such teachers will give you a similar picture to that which I myself am now giving you, to the effect that there is no universal compulsory reincarnation but that reincarnation is possible. There may be – I believe there is – a school of thought which teaches compulsory reincarnation but there again, as we have discussed many times, the mind of man incarnate is a peculiar thing and it will seize upon a facet of a truth and proceed to elaborate it and to enlarge upon it until it fills the whole horizon. And so, whilst the general idea of reincarnation is, as I have said, perfectly feasible and perfectly intelligible, it is not the case that all spirit *must* reincarnate. It is not indeed the fact that all spirit *must* become incarnate at all.

The picture is bigger, it is broader, it is wider than any such concept would allow, do you see?

Questioner. We are specks in the universe.

Abu. Even, my sister, in the universe of which you have knowledge. Indeed and indeed, I have said many times – I have said and it must always be the burden of my speaking – that God is greater than you or I or any individual can comprehend. And man, even man incarnate, can, to a large degree, comprehend his present universe; therefore God must transcend that universe – as indeed He does, but I give it to you in terms of logic, and so it were parochial to say or to suggest that there is the little ball which you name the Earth – there are a few thousand, a few million (I do not know) souls who are dwelling upon the earth . . . and that is Creation . . . that is God . . . there is nothing more! These spirits, the spirits of those persons dwelling upon earth, will pass to a spirit-plane . . . and that is still all that there is; and that they will proceed and progress until eventually *they* shall merge with the God-head . . . and that is all there is of the God-head!

I ask you, my friends, my children, I ask you to contemplate the picture! It will not do. For God is vaster than any comprehension and His love embraces the whole of His creation, not alone that upon the earth.

And so, God is love and love is God and love is all – all that you know and all that you do not know and all that we – including myself – *cannot* know, but one day will, when we shall comprehend that love.

With all blessing I leave you.

Chapter Twenty-Nine

THE 'GREAT ONES'

Questioner. You told us that to some degree those you have called the 'Great Ones' play a part in the moulding of our lives. You yourself and others with you make 'missionary' journeys to us whilst those still close to the earth naturally play a part in influencing and helping us, but what about the multitudinous spirits who are, so to speak, in between? Do many of them still interest themselves in this world and, if so, how do they show it?

Abu. I thank you for your question but I am not quite clear as to the meaning of 'in between', for, as I think you have been told by another communicator, there are a series of what have been termed 'natural stations' upon which the spirit of man can and shall sojourn for a time, greater or lesser according to his desire and to his advancement, and the in-between regions, not being natural stations, are not positions of contentment and those who may dwell in between will hardly be applying their minds to circumstances other than their own, for the time being at least. It is not until the spirit shall arrive upon a 'natural station', where it shall feel at home and shall have for the time being no aspiration to rise beyond that state – for the time being always – that it can or will turn its attention downwards (if I may use the term) even as far as the earth-plane. But perhaps that was not the purport of your question.

Questioner. I think that I can perhaps make clearer what I had in mind. I picture the 'Great Ones' in a region that is, by your own words, beyond your own 'natural station' if I may so call it, but there must be many 'natural stations' or resting places inhabited by the innumerable spirits who have left the earth over greatly varying periods of time. Do they in any way influence what goes on here?

Abu. To a degree, yes, there is influencing, there is 'interference', as it were, with the mental and spiritual affairs of earth from any and all of the spiritual levels, the levels of advancement between the stage upon which dwells our dear friend Alfred and others and that whereon find themselves those whom I have designated the 'Great Ones', who are so remote that it is a little difficult to refer to them as persons or individuals, and therefore such influence as they shall exert will be of a more general nature and less individualised for that reason as you will understand. And, as one shall descend down the scale, so the impact shall become more and more personal and individual – that necessarily follows.

My own teachings, which I endeavour to put before you, are and always have been, as you will agree, of a general nature. I have, admittedly, addressed a specific body of the children for it is only by such means that any message can be brought to the earth-plane, but my message has always been of general application and, in so far as it has been possible, I have avoided specific references, except when called upon to assist or to aid, perhaps, in some personal matter and there, my heart being touched, I have endeavoured to do what I could perhaps do in the matter, but that is not to say that it is my habit of mind, shall I say, to poke a finger into the various pies upon the earth-plane of which I may have knowledge. Whereas, when one shall come down to the next stage of life, upon which people like our friend Alfred now dwell, his interests, his concerns, will certainly be as specifically individual as they were when he was himself encased in flesh, for he is not far enough advanced from the earth-plane to be able to take the broader, wider view which follows necessarily upon advancement. Therefore, the general, broad issues with which the 'Great Ones' deal – with which I myself endeavour to deal – would be too broad and too wide perhaps to have value or real meaning in the eyes and to the spirit of such a one as the one we are speaking of. Does that assist you at all or have I still left some matters untouched?

Questioner. There is still one point on which I am not clear. You referred to natural stations and said that only when something in the nature of a natural station was reached, where a spirit would function at ease, would that spirit be likely to renew its interest in the earth. Am I right in suggesting, as I did, that there are many such stations? I have no wish to 'enumerate'.

Abu. Many such stations – yes indeed, but how far are you wishful to go? Many, many, many such stations, but, commencing with the earth-plane up to for example my own (as you will recall, I am within the fourth heaven!) – for the sake of this particular argument we will say that, from the earth-plane up to the sphere or plane upon which I myself have my being, there are, shall we say, four planes existent. I will not be precise upon the point because it is a graduation, as you have been told – there are graduations between the spheres – but there are stations upon that line which are *natural* stations.

I will touch upon a subject known a little to me though not strictly within my sphere. In the scientific world you have, I believe, a picture of the construction of your material atoms which, as I am informed consist of a central body, a nucleus, surrounded by planetary forces or electrons and these electrons are in a state of motion round the central nucleus. They can rotate only in certain orbits and, to pass from one orbit to another, they must quite evidently depass the space between the orbits – and therefore be in *existence* between the orbits – whilst unable normally to function between those orbits. That is the state of those who are in between natural stations. They are in process of rising (or falling, for the spirit of man *can* fall if it so wish after death) and whilst in the process of rising are virtually unable, because of that process of rising, to do other than *rise*. And, having arisen and attained their new orbit or natural station, they will sojourn there for a while, possibly for a very long while, for time, as we are all too well aware, has different meanings to different dwellers upon different spheres. And then attention can and will be given to matters other than their own immediate progression or advancement or 'rising'. Does that help at all?

Questioner. Yes, it certainly does, but you say "attention can be given". I am wishful to know if it is likely to be given. Has the earth by that time become for most of them so remote and so outside their sphere that, in fact, attention would not be given?

Abu. There is recollection of earth for quite a long time but there is very, very much less of the missionary effort which I myself and others with me are making by comparison with those who are content and satisfied to have left behind the earth and all that it has meant, and the succeeding spheres also and all that *they* have meant. There is much less missionary work than there is recollection: it is not necessary that all who have a recollection of their earth-life shall turn their attention again to earth. And so, without endeavouring to go into numbers, for it would not be possible for me so to do, I would say that a relatively small proportion of those in the upper spheres turn their attention sufficiently to the earth to be desirous of returning thereto, and, the higher one shall go, the less is that attention given.

Questioner. But, for those who do not wish to make a missionary journey back, as you have done, are there any possibilities of influencing us, except in the general way in which all spirit beings are in touch with us – who are also spirit beings. Are there any specific ways of operating?

Abu. Individually, no – not in general terms. If the attention, the mind, of a spirit person, dwelling perhaps – it matters not – upon the very next plane of life, is not turned directly earthwards, then the influencing is negligible and consists, as you have suggested, only of the general influence which the spirit world endeavours to exercise upon the earth-plane. But again, it does not matter how far removed from the earth-plane a spirit person may be, if he has the missionary intent and the missionary desire, then he *will* turn his attention towards the earth and he will use such endeavour as he can bring to bear to influence the earth.

In that connection you will recall what I have already said about the potential ability of spirit teachers – spirit people such as myself, for example – when dwelling upon our own plane, as compared with that which we are able to put into exercise when we again return to the earth. The desire to influence may be very much greater than the ability to influence.

Questioner. Do most of the teachers who speak through mediums come from nearer to earth?

Abu. No, my sister, I would prefer to think that most of the teachers come from the plane or sphere or upon which I myself dwell. For, lower than that, insufficient has been learned and absorbed and, higher than that, it becomes progressively more and more difficult to effect this particular return. I have already expressed my own state as being a kind of halfway between the Great Ones and the earth-plane (again, you will not tie me down to linear measurements!) in that sense it is about "half-way". There are Indian guides, there are Chinese guides, there are Egyptians and of course there are white English guides also – controls, guides, teachers – who have advanced and who have learned and reached a stage where they are able to teach and a stage *from which* they are *able* to teach – for the two must go together.

You spoke a little while ago about the possibility of a spirit having been within the spirit-world "for a long time". I must disabuse your mind of that idea for it does not matter how long or how short a time a person has been in spirit, divorced from flesh: it is purely and solely a question of spiritual advancement. There are those upon your earth-plane here and now who, upon their transition, upon their shedding the physical envelope, will advance and progress through the spheres very rapidly indeed and will join me and others with me upon my own plane and will commence within a very short earth time a series of endeavours to teach which you might think befitted only a spirit who has been in the spirit-world for a very long time. But the length of time has nothing to do with it, it is purely a question of spiritual advancement.

I have said that there are those upon the earth-plane who in sleep visit what we have agreed to call without confusion the 'Christ sphere', and that sphere is the sphere to which I and others go upon a pilgrimage, and you will gather that it is as vastly removed from my own domicile as is that from the earth-plane. But there are those upon the earth-plane who visit that Christ sphere in their sleep and who, upon shedding the physical body, will speedily pass through the planes and the spheres. They will not go there 'in one leap' for that cannot be, but they will pass speedily through, absorbing what must be absorbed in the way of appreciation of the life of spirit as they go, until they shall dwell *there*; then they may or may not keep attention upon the earth-plane – that is a matter for individual preference.

Questioner. Those who actually go in their sleep as far as you have just told us – do they benefit by it?

Abu. My child, the point does not arise. If they shall travel thereto that is their natural station here and now. We others, I myself, our dear friend Alfred, going upon a pilgrimage to places such as this which are not our natural stations, will benefit – of course we shall benefit – but those who visit the Christ sphere because of their spiritual advancement, which fits them for such habitation, have no need of additional benefit therefrom – it *is* their natural station.

Questioner. I was thinking of those who go to that sphere to gain strength.

Abu. Indeed and indeed – to gain strength. Again to let my eyes rest (I speak metaphorically, of course) upon the glory of the sight of a realm where the love of God is so vastly manifest by comparison with the manifestations which can exist further down the scale – for there is a dimming and a darkening, as I have already told you, and it cannot be otherwise. The golden thread is there, yes indeed, to the very lowest, the very bottom most pit of all, the golden thread is there still. But we are now speaking of a realm where the warmth and the light would be unbearable were we not conditioned for a time to enjoy it, to be revivified and rejuvenated and strengthened and refreshed by it, when we shall return to our own habitation and again when I shall descend here to the earth-plane, bringing as I trust a little dim reflection of the glory which I have been permitted to gaze upon. Of course we are helped, of course we are aided and refreshed, and that is the purpose of the pilgrimage; and the pilgrimage is made possible for all aspiring souls who will and who can benefit from it; that is the only test: there is none other.

I do not speak – I have never spoken – of planes beyond the Christ sphere wherein dwell the Great Ones, for beyond such spheres one enters into conditions which I do not think the human mind, as constituted both on earth and in myself, could fully grasp, and so there would be no point in endeavouring to speak of such circumstances, for the words would have no meaning.

I have given you an imagery of the countless, endless spheres and planes, going on and on to this infinity, which is God, but we must be content not to endeavour to draw a picture of such, for it will be apparent to you that, by the mere act of reduplication of wonder, of light, of warmth and of glory, one must eventually come to a transcendental state which cannot be described or imagined, and that is so.

In my own experience what I have called the Christ sphere is the highest and the furthest of the spheres which an earth mind can be expected firmly to grasp – a sphere which has and will have meaning for the mind and to which therefore those still dwelling upon earth, as I have just said, can safely be taken. Beyond that, I think not: there would be but bewilderment until after long sojourn upon such a sphere the spirit should have transcended earthly logic and reason and limitation and become able to enter into transcendental conditions which, by virtue of being transcendental, cannot even be discussed. But we do not need to go as far, for our image has led us to the God who is love. And the love is the same no matter upon what sphere it is manifested: it is the same love.

Chapter Thirty

THE PROCESS KNOWN AS RESCUE WORK

Questioner. How or why is it that people have to be brought for us to help when apparently they could so much more easily be helped by those on your side?

Abu. The greater mystery, I would have thought, was the possibility of their being influenced, of their being brought at all, when, as is rightly claimed, we are unable ourselves to make a contact with them. How then is it possible that we can *bring* them: that must seem to be quite a contradiction to you.

Questioner. The one sounds like some sort of mental contact and the other of a different order.

2nd Questioner. I think it is an automatic process. When you see a 'light' you see something which you naturally go towards.

Questioner. But if so one would suppose there must be a miscellaneous and enormous crowd of such persons whereas, in fact, only certain people come to us.

Abu. My child has the stick by the right end, at least to a degree, for, as she rightly says, those who are bewildered and lost and wandering in semi-darkness will see a light and from sheer curiosity, if from nothing else, may make towards the light they see; but it is not all those there who *can* see a light. It is a figure of speech, an imagery, but the actual directing of those ones who are to be brought to you in order that you may endeavour to help them is done by the Great Ones, not by any lesser ones. None less could so influence them for, in such a state and at such a time, they are not competent to stand upon their own feet, their own spiritual feet, and none lesser than the Great Ones could permit themselves to exercise such influence.

Questioner. One feels inclined to ask why, if the 'Great Ones' are capable of doing such a thing, they do not do the rest of the job, so to speak. Is it the fact that there is a fundamental law which their action is only 'implementing' as it were and that it has to be so?

Abu. Quite evidently it has to be so for so it is. As you have said, there is the Law but I cannot enter into the question of why the Law is as it is, yet I do not wish to hide behind such a reply. Those spirits who are the Great Ones I have claimed exercise direction by means of influence, mental and spiritual influence, in so far as they are able and in so far as those upon earth are receptive, and these unhappy ones of whom we are now speaking are to all intents and purposes still upon the earth-plane. The fact that they have shed the physical envelope matters little or nothing. As far as we are concerned – I and the greater ones than I – it matters little or nothing, and those who are dead, yet not freed, are in the same position in our eyes as those who in your eyes are not yet dead and are subject to some form of influencing.

126

Now if any one of you shall throw himself or herself open, deliberately and wittingly, by means of the exercise of what we will call prayer (I will not baulk at the word) to the influence of one of us, that prayer, that appeal, will, as I have already said, reach the 'level' which is appropriate to its nature and its content and will reach the one for whom it is 'intended', and it will be responded to, in so far as it is possible to respond, in terms of influence and inspiration. But if you shall not so open your heart and your mind and make yourselves receptive to influence and inspiration from us, must that mean then that you are completely shut off from such influencing? No, but the influence must come from further away, from higher up, from a more powerful source, and it will be the more impersonal therefore.

That is the position, because these unhappy ones of whom we now speak, possibly even unaware that they have left the earth life and should not still be haunting the surface of the earth-plane, will not be receptive to inspiration or influencing from such as we are, because they will not open themselves to that influence since they do not know of it and possibly do not even admit of it. But they may not be shut off and lost therefore, and this spiritual influencing, whilst being far more impersonal, is none the less powerful, and so they are guided, they are inspired, they are influenced, without their own knowledge – very frequently without their own knowledge at all – to 'follow the light', as my child has put it. Occasionally they may actually think that they see a light, for the emanations from a medium when in trance and sitting in circle such as this will quite frequently resemble a light in the eyes of those who *need* a light. We do not need a light, but for those who do need a light, the light is provided; for in such a state the spiritual factualities will present themselves in a manner acceptable to the mind of the one who is seeking, and that is why a light is seen when in fact no light exists. It is not a light by which you could burn your finger but it is a light as far as this one is concerned, and if it must appear to be a physical or semi-physical light before he shall be attracted thereto, very well, there is no difficulty at all about creating that, and then this one shall approach closer to this light and shall find himself within the sphere of influence of a circle of sitters such as those and shall then, without his own knowledge, place himself as it were, under the orders and under the control of those who are even now regulating the affairs of this very circle, and this one shall find himself addressed by and speaking to people in the same condition as he himself has been.

It is paralled by the circumstances upon earth: I know it has a 'ghostly' appearance, I know that it must appear at times to you to have an unreality, but it is paralled upon earth. If you should perhaps unfortunately suffer a lapse of memory – an amnesia is it not? – you will not know for a time who you are, where you are, where you are going, who are these people whom you meet in the street. You will then approach someone who can help you, you will ask someone, where am I, what is the day, what is the year; you will endeavour to orientate yourself, to find out where you are, what has happened and what you can do to get back into your own orbit, is it not so? It would be a reasonable thing to do, and if you shall address those who cannot help you, being in the same state as yourself, you will not get very far. But if one of those shall, being a little more knowledgeable than the others perhaps, take you by the arm and say: I can take you to a place, perhaps a police station or some other bureau of assistance where they will be able to assist by probing into all kinds of things, and you shall be led into this place of assistance and questions shall be put to you and you shall put questions to those who are there from which shall emerge answers to your questions and your difficulties which shall give you some satisfaction, then you have a parallel case to that of those unhappy ones who are brought to you.

Questioner. I have experienced this myself. I had lost my memory (only for a short time) but I was, I think, at that time too terrified of meeting somebody who should discover that I did not know·anything to go and ask questions from, and this same state might be comparable. You build up a barrier, fearing to be told something that you don't want to hear. I knew nothing of where I was, I could not remember anything at all; I could see people but nothing would have induced me to ask anybody about anything. I think perhaps these people build up an even bigger barrier of the same kind.

Abu. Out of the mouths of babes and sucklings! There is no occasion for me to enlarge upon this matter for here my child has had this same experience whilst still encased in the flesh.

Questioner. We have had quite a number of such people visit this circle from time to time; were these people directed or did they by chance see the 'light'?

Abu. It is very seldom that a meeting such as this is blundered into 'by chance', for you see, if that were frequently possible, then undoubtedly your meetings would be disrupted much more frequently; but you have a wall of power, you have a barrier of protection, which is erected round a gathering such as this in order that it may remain untarnished and unattacked; for not all those who are in need of help are aware of the fact and not all those who are in need of help are nice people whom it would be possible at the moment to help. Some of them we have called evil: I have preferred the term unworthy, but from your point of view they would be evil ones, so it would not be at all kindly on the part of the operators who make possible these communications if they were to leave open all kinds of doors through which all and sundry might come and disrupt your circle and your sitting, though on occasion it does occur, as you will perhaps be aware. So that, in general, those who come before you are under a degree of mental compulsion.

Questioner. They are selected, so to speak, and allowed to come in?

Abu. Yes, they are selected, but they are selected by the operation of the Great Ones and that is an impersonal selection. They are not selected because they have such and such a countenance or they are of such and such a height; they are selected, but the selection is an automatic selection; they are selected generally because they, those who are brought, are as it were, 'ripe' for helping and it is seldom that an error is made.

Questioner. Why is it that some come and then do not return?

Abu. Because, generally speaking, happily you have succeeded in achieving your object. I can but say that the proof of the pudding is in the eating. If one shall come and shall perhaps even be objectionable (for I know that this can occur upon occasion) you shall speak words to this one, words intended to be helpful; you shall request perhaps that this one shall return again to you in order that he or she may be yet more advised and helped and educated, and yet this one does not so return. You are not to think of that as a failure and a loss but quite the reverse. The strong probability is that you have actually opened a chink within this mind which, whilst it may not have succeeded in completing the work which you have begun, will have enabled those in spirit now to make a contact and finish the work, for we would not wish to overload you. We in spirit, as I have told you before, are potentially more powerful indeed, when we can come to grips, but it is you who must crack such shells first, and it is seldom that you and we jointly fail completely. If it were an evil-minded person it is doubtful whether the Great Ones would have influenced him to approach you in the first place, for they will know what I cannot know.

Questioner. Of course the protracted realisation that there is something better and the slow, painful steps taken towards it are, as I see it, really the influencing of the Great Ones or the working out of the Law: these two are not, I imagine, separable.

Abu. The actions, mental and spiritual, of the Great Ones are of course the working of the Law. The Laws are not laid down by the Great Ones but the Great Ones have quite a lot to do with the working of the Law. They cannot set the Law aside but they can use the Law and they do, and of course they will use you, as they do use you; they will use us, as they do use us. Our friend Alfred has told you upon occasion that he gets his 'orders' . . . It is true that he gets his orders indeed; he may not know whence they come but I know whence they come: they come from the Great Ones, and Alfred is being influenced mentally and spiritually quite directly though in an impersonal manner by the Great Ones in exactly the same way as you are influenced, sometimes directly by the Great Ones, not always by lesser individuals but sometimes directly by the Great Ones where matters of real moment are involved – matters of spiritual moment. I trust you will now have a better appreciation of the circumstances attending those who have passed over with little or no information and knowledge.

They are not wicked people, very few of them are wicked people, but their eyes are closed and blind: they are spiritually blind. It is the very sad and regrettable state of the earth-world that so many people are in that condition, and, since following the death of the physical body they will exist in a spirit condition, it is necessary that they may be able to see with their spirit eyes and as a baby upon the earth must learn to see, must learn to focus, to recognise and collate and tabulate, so must the spirit of man learn to do these things. But he is spirit here and now whilst encased in the flesh and he has opportunity here and now of learning of his spirit origin and his spirit being and, if he will but do that and endeavour to open ever so little his spiritual eyes whilst still in the flesh, he will have done his baby learning before he shall pass over and he will save himself

129

much bewilderment and sometimes much distress by learning, in so far as he can from people such as yourselves who have contacted people such as us, of the circumstances following upon earthly death, and it eases the passage considerably and it eases very considerably our work too if this work can be done whilst these people are still living upon the earth-plane as ordinary men and women.

(This subject was taken up again at a later date and a similar question was put to Abu. Since a fresh light was thrown on it by his answer, it is printed here following on his earlier reply.)

Questioner. We regret that so few of the numberless spirits coming over in ignorance can be helped by us, when the need must be so great.

Abu. You are suffering, and quite naturally, under the time limitation of your earth-world. May I recall to you that it is not very long ago that there was but one or perhaps two men living upon your earth-plane who knew that the sun does not go round the earth. There are few now who do not know this. Have no fear, this is God's work, there are many hands; there are more hands than you can be aware of engaged upon this work.

If you will but refrain from commencing another bloody war and hurtling souls in their thousands, in their hundreds of thousands, unprepared, vengeful, bewildered, shocked, injured and hurt, into a plane unable to receive them because unable to contact them owing to their mental barriers. I pray you – your endeavours must be but puny in this particular respect – but I beg of you that such thought-power as you can exercise, such prayer as you find yourselves capable of, shall be directed "into the blue", that all, whether incarnate or discarnate, who may receive that thought-form of yours may be impelled and impressed, in so far as it may be, to work against another catastrophe such as a further war upon the plane of earth would be.

Leave the situation as it now is and it is sufficiently calamitous, for you have upon the earth manifold accidental passings to our plane, many of which could be avoided and so we – those of us who are engaged in this work – have more to do than we can compass at times, though not more than we are willing to do, not more than we have the *potentiality* to do, but more than we are able to do because of the condition of the minds which are sent to us. But at least you are not then sending spirits heavenward in their hundreds of thousands in the fiery state of bewilderment which so many of them must arrive in during the course of a war. That apart, have no fear; the work proceeds and it will proceed.

You have been told in the past that much work has been going on and still goes on upon the spirit planes at all levels to endeavour to avoid a further armed conflict upon the earth. We shall continue those efforts, we shall redouble those efforts for we are concerned and perturbed about the situation, and that is why I beg that you will give thought upon occasion to that situation – the situation of world peace upon the earth. A further war would set back this goodly work by a long, long period. We should not be frustrated, we should not be defeated; we should merely have to redouble our efforts, but it has been and it would be again, a set-back that would take a considerable degree of surmounting.

(At a later date another communicator (known to us as "Andrews") gave us the following explanation of what happens when a concentration of thought is

130

directed upon any particular soul who may be supposed to have passed to spirit life in a condition of ignorance or bewilderment.)

Mr. Andrews. If a person passes from the earth life with no knowledge of the life following on physical death, there is apt to be a degree of bewilderment and mental confusion; and since, as you will understand, the circumstances and conditions which one inhabits following upon physical death are so very strongly influenced by the mind of the individual, anyone coming over here in such circumstances will find themselves, quite frequently, in what appears to be an actual fog or darkness. The fog or darkness is peculiar to themselves; they will be actually on the same plane or stage as many other people not in such a condition, but this darkness or fog is peculiar to them. Then, a concentration by well-meaning people such as yourselves, directed as actively as you can towards some individual (and be it noted, the individual must be as it were indicated – preferably of course by personal knowledge) has the effect of shining something in the nature of a light or a searchlight upon this individual soul who is in darkness, and that enables those of us who are interested in any particular case to pick this person out from surrounding patches of darkness, because there are a number of people who do pass over in such unfortunate conditions. It 'spotlights', as it were, the individual to whom you refer.

I would also mention in passing that that is the explanation – in case you have ever sought for one – as to why people sometimes in dire need of help are brought along to a circle such as yours so that they may be helped. You will not have thought of them because of course you will have had no knowledge of them, but *someone* has, someone thought of these people – generally speaking from the side of earth – and those people have been spotlighted so far as we are concerned and it has then become possible for those on the spirit side who give themselves to this particular work to influence them, to persuade them, and bring them as it were along to you. It might have seemed perhaps that the process was rather like "picking out winners with a pin", but it is not like that at all. These people who have been brought to you have been first brought to our attention by some such process as that which you have just been carrying out. Unfortunately I cannot say that it is *always* effective because to some extent it depends upon the state of mind and whether it is at all receptive, of the person concerned. For if someone comes across to the spirit side with a mind resolutely closed, then I am afraid even your searchlight cannot illuminate that one, but in general terms that is the position. You, as it were, put a spotlight on this one for whom you are seeking help and thereafter *we* are in a better position to give such help, in whatever direction it can be given, direct from spirit or, alternatively, through people like yourselves.

I am sure you will forgive me for intruding, but I do like to feel,when it is possible, that when you people here on earth are called upon by one of your leaders on earth or in spirit to perform certain ceremonial "rites" as they may appear to be, that it is as well you should have the underlying reason for such things. You sit and "concentrate" – very well; it may pass through the minds of some of the people who are concentrating to ask what exactly they are doing and why they are doing it and what effect it can have, and I thought you might be interested to know.

THE ABU TAPES

A series of cassette tape recordings are available from The Abu Trust. They cover many interesting and varied subjects. You can now hear the actual 'voices', as they were recorded during the Norman Hunt 'circle sittings', of the wonderful teacher ABU (meaning Father) plus other communicators from the realms of spirit.

ALF (doorkeeper to the circle) was a London cockney when on earth and speaks with ease and humour but with such wisdom. BLACK HAWK helps with rescue work, ANDREWS is a chemist, BARTHOLOMEW a scientist and DR. CHANG discusses healing.

These recordings will help to answer most, if not all, of your enquiring questions and will provide a great deal to talk about and think over, and could certainly change your whole outlook on life and daily living!

For further information write (enclosing a stamp) to:

The Abu Trust,
"Woodside",
Canadia Road,
Battle,
E. Sussex,
TN33 0LR.